Tan. Diamonds 1311

Quotes Al

[handwritten] 47 Being Values ... [handwritten] 6 1 ... now

". . . one of the best interviewers who has ever worked the American airwaves, radio or TV."

Robert Fuller
Physicist, educator, past president of Oberlin College,
and active citizen diplomat

"Someone with whom I have cruised some important realms of the cosmic ocean and in doing so have developed ever increasing confidence in his intuitive navigation."

R. Buckminster Fuller (1895–1983)
Inventor of the geodesic dome, designer,
philosopher, and creator of the World Game

". . . Bill Moyers and Michael Toms are alike: two of the most creative interviewers it has been my good fortune to work with."

Joseph Campbell (1904–1987)
Mythologist and author of *Hero with a Thousand Faces*, *The Masks of God*, *Myths to Live By*, and *The Mythic Image*

[handwritten notes] Definitive own vision of success
High level of vitality — Smith
Me - openness of time + space, flow, cute, beauty, connection, deep, soulful, rich

[handwritten] 93 dolphins + whales - save the wilderness

New Dimensions Books

Marsha Sinetar
in Conversation with
Michael Toms

Series editor
Hal Zina Bennett

Published by

Aslan Publishing
Lower Lake, California
USA

Published by
Aslan Publishing
P.O. Box 108
Lower Lake, CA 95457
(707) 995-1861

For a free catalog of all our titles,
or to order more copies of this book
please call (800) 275-2606

Library of Congress Cataloging-in-Publication Data

Sinetar, Marsha
    Marsha Sinetar in conversation with Michael Toms.
        p. cm. — (New dimensions books)
    ISBN 0-944031-39-0 : $8.95
    1. Sinetar, Marsha—Interviews. 2. Psychologists—United
States—Interviews. 3. Success—Psychological aspects. 4. Self-
actualization (Psychology) 5. Work—Psychological aspects.
I. Toms, Michael. II. Title. III. Series: New dimensions books
(Lower Lake, Calif.)
BF109.S47A5 1993
158--dc20
                                                            93-5908
                                                            CIP

Printed in USA

10 9 8 7 6 5 4 3 2 1

Table of Contents

Introduction

Following your dream, or really doing what you love, falls into the realm of fantasy or bad fiction for most people. A recent survey showed that seventy-five percent of those questioned didn't like their jobs and would prefer to be doing something else. When we are children, all possibilities exist—from astronaut to fireman, from artist to playwright—and then, somewhere along the way, career looms large and society tells us by example what we're supposed to do with our life—namely, join the crowd and fall in line without questioning the process. The path is seductive and like quicksand; it swallows you whole.

Yet some people are able to escape being mired in the mundane. They follow their heart, no matter what anyone says or thinks, and live creative, full and happy lives, oftentimes without fanfare or acknowledgment. No longer do they define themselves by what they do; rather, they can be recognized by who they are.

So it was that I first encountered Marsha Sinetar through her book *Ordinary People as Monks and Mystics,* and then learned that she lived not far away from where I resided, on the Northern California coast. We became friends, and I came to understand that she was not just working as a writer but was actively engaged in "following her bliss." At the time she was writing *Do What You Love, The Money Will Follow,* which, after being published, became a national bestseller and brought much acclaim to Marsha.

One of those rare individuals whose actions match her words, she is very much a hermit, but through her writings has been able to share her insights about life and living. She believes that how we experience life is closely related to the choices we make on a day-to-day basis. What we choose today creates what we experience tomorrow, and these choices must come from the deepest part of ourselves. As we work more deeply with the inner and are able to choose creatively, the outer is transformed in direct proportion to that process. Through the choices we make, Marsha feels, we can learn how to live in a way that encourages self-esteem, self-respect and joy in who we are.

Her philosophy is based on fundamental truths and spiritual values. She believes that we can attain happiness and that it may, indeed, be far greater than the simplistic promise of the traditional fairy tale. The way we perceive may produce the world we actually experience. Problems become opportunities, and obstacles are merely new challenges to catalyze our creative power and express the best within us. This is some of the credo of Marsha Sinetar, a contemplative in a fast-paced world of busy-ness and distractions, someone who offers us another way of being—a way of simplicity, compassion and true creativity.

Michael Toms
Ukiah, California
July 1993

▲

Section One

▼

Right Living
and Making Money Too

The title of Marsha Sinetar's book *Do What You Love, The Money Will Follow* captures the essence of her message. Something in that title strikes a chord in all of us. We all want to be able to make a living doing what we most enjoy doing. But is that really possible?

Doing what you really love can seem, above all else, like an unattainable fantasy. Why else would seventy-five percent of those who were asked in a *Fortune* magazine survey admit that they didn't like their jobs and would prefer to be doing something else? When asked why they didn't change jobs, most expressed the belief that one shouldn't expect much more than a paycheck as the reward for work. "Making a living is a necessary evil," seemed to be the overriding sentiment most people expressed where their work was concerned.

Marsha Sinetar says it doesn't have to be that way—that it is possible to do what we really love and make a good living at it, too.

The dreams of discovering our right livelihood start very early in life for most of us. But sadly, these are dreams which too quickly die. When we are children, everything seems possible. The world is filled with dreams and we believe we can be anything we want to be, from astronaut to fireman, from artist to playwright, from math teacher to scientist. But somewhere along the way our career choices become an issue and instead of following our dreams we choose our future vocations according to what society directs.

In one way or another, many of us have chosen our vocations according to pressures from family or peers. Or we chose what appeared to be promising opportunities in the outside world, rather than looking within ourselves; too many of us abandon our dreams like the toys of our childhood, treating them as if they were no longer relevant.

The many employment opportunities that are offered to us in our late teens and early twenties are indeed enticing, and even seductive. And, of course, economic necessity motivates many of us to get into jobs or professions we don't like. In any case, all too many of us find ourselves trapped in money-making activities that threaten to swallow us whole.

In Marsha Sinetar's books, workshops and lectures, we clearly learn that it doesn't have to be this way. She tells us of people who are able to escape getting mired down in work that isn't satisfying to them. She tells of people who follow their hearts, no matter what, living creative, fulfilling and happy lives, oftentimes without fanfare or acknowledgment.

She tells of people who define themselves not according to what they do but according to who they are.

• • •

MICHAEL: Marsha, when did you start following your dreams? What is your own story about the role of work in your life?

MARSHA: Ever since I was a child, I have felt a little bit out of step with the rest of the world, mostly because of an intensity about my work that transforms whatever I do almost into play. Growing up, I realized that this was something that not everyone felt. Now it's different; I have a sweet group of friends around me who seem to share a similar attitude toward work.

In the early days, when I was teaching, I noticed that many colleagues couldn't wait for the weekend, when they could at last leave their work behind and enjoy life. Or they spent the nine-month school year groaning about their responsibilities and counting the days until summer vacation when they could start enjoying their lives. That was a big surprise to me; I couldn't imagine how people could ever get to the point of hating their work that much.

Early on I also became aware of a small, high-spirited group who enjoyed whatever they were doing, and especially their work or studies. Everything about their lives seemed more vital, more alive than those who hated their work. And that intrigued me so much that I actually began studying what made these individuals so unique, so different from the rest.

At first my study was very informal. Then I started keeping notes. First these were mental notes. Then they were short scribblings in a journal. Then, along with my professional practice, I listened carefully to interviews I was conducting—interviews with people who were successful and also with people who weren't.

I had my own criteria for what I meant by success. I didn't mean just monetary success. Rather, I was searching for that vitality that shone through those who loved their work. Why was it there? What did it mean? And then about ten years ago I realized that there was probably a book in all this, one that could be tremendously helpful in answering people's questions about work satisfaction and following their dreams.

That's how the study began. As soon as I visualized it as a book I began to interview people I'd identified as having transcended their work so that it became like play.

MICHAEL: I'm always amazed at how people stay in work that isn't pleasurable, that they don't enjoy in any way. What are some of the reasons for that? Are there any specific characteristics of people who stay in something that they don't like doing?

MARSHA: There are whole clusters of reasons. There are those who are simply immature, who for one reason or another are not willing to engage with life so as to have a good time. They may have the ideal job for them, but they are unwilling to embrace it and receive pleasure from it, just as they are not willing to fully enjoy life. It's all the same, you know, work-life and personal-life; these two—work and life—can't be separated. We can't really compartmentalize them.

If you've ever worked in a large, structured organization with many other people, you've probably observed that there are those people who don't like their work because they have selected it unconsciously; they've gotten their job by default, as it were, and it has little or nothing to do with who they are. That's another type of person, distinct from the immature—someone who has not consciously selected their occupation.

A third type is the person who hasn't the self-esteem to reach out for what they would truly enjoy. This type of person knows what he or she really wants but cannot for the life of them imagine being "lucky" enough to land a job in that field.

So those are three main types and three key reasons that people remain in jobs they dislike: immaturity, making unconscious employment-choices and lack of self-esteem.

MICHAEL: What about feeling locked into a job because of financial pressures or rewards? We all know people who say, well, I couldn't possibly do what I really want to do because I couldn't earn the money that I am making now, or I wouldn't have an insurance program, or I wouldn't have a guaranteed expense account, or I wouldn't have my company car.

MARSHA: Yes...such persons think, "I couldn't possibly get the job I want where I want to live," or "I have these several responsibilities... I have wife or a husband... a family to support... kids to put through school." Or "I haven't the proper education and can't earn a degree because I'm working." There are a million different rationalizations.

In my interviews I discovered hundreds of people who spelled out all the reasons they didn't like their work and all of the reasons why they couldn't change it. Most of them felt trapped, as I've said. They gave the situation more power than they were willing to give themselves. They were saying, in effect, "I don't have the personal power to extricate myself from that situation."

MICHAEL: Can we escape the trap?

MARSHA: Yes. We can always escape the trap. For example, people who really thrive in their work, who have the vitality I spoke about, aren't necessarily individuals with more money or education or opportunities than the rest of us; that's not what gives them that dynamism. They may even face some of the same so-called traps any of the rest of us do: too many children, high living expenses, lack of schooling and so on. They may not reside in the ideal geographic location to do the thing they want to do. Or they could have some physical handicap. And yet they are able to do their chosen vocation because they consciously create the situations to actualize it.

I suggest that almost any problem, anything that appears to be an impediment or a handicap, can be worked through.

If we really want something badly enough we will figure out a way to get it, to make it happen.

I am not saying that there are never any trade-offs. Usually there are. And I am not implying that if one has many children, or a physical handicap, or lacks the required education or even the talent to do what they prefer, that there won't be hardships or adjustments that must be made. No matter what our situation, there are dues to be paid. But I also observe that we can structure things in our favor, as Joseph Chilton Pierce wrote in his book *The Crack in the Cosmic Egg.*

We can structure working conditions in our favor and many people do. Tom Peters, the organizational consultant, once noted that, there are one hundred million people in the workplace. And as the study you quoted at the beginning of this interview indicated, seventy-five percent of these people are unhappy in their work. That still leaves twenty-five percent who have figured out how to do something they enjoy. And that's a lot of people!

MICHAEL: I wonder how often we get into the right work, that is, the work which we thoroughly enjoy, where we experience this vitality you describe, by accident. I was thinking about the time I left a corporation where I had worked for a long time. I really thought I couldn't get a job in advertising because I didn't have the experience or the background or whatever. The only way I thought I could get into the advertising business was to create my own business, be my own employer. And that's what I did. So it was like doing the right thing by mistake, or maybe even for the wrong reasons.

It wasn't until much later that I got the idea that, well, maybe I really could do whatever I wanted to if only I put my attention to it.

MARSHA: Let's look more closely at this. The desire you had to accomplish all this suggests to me that your eventual success was no accident. What was an accident, if there is such a thing, and sometimes it seems there isn't, is that you didn't know you couldn't do it. Now, you apparently didn't learn these "impossibility lessons" well in school. If you had learned them you would have been convinced that you couldn't succeed unless you had the formal education or the financial resources, or whatever. Schools usually convince us that we must have this or that degree, and we must have business connections and "family ties." I guess you forgot to listen that day.

MICHAEL: I was just remembering that in college my major was radio, television and film. The university I attended had a graduate department in that field. The first class I took was in radio. The professor opened the class by telling us that all the major networks combined had only two jobs available for college graduates of the previous year... like, no one gets a job in this field once they get out of college. And of course, I never got a job with one of the big broadcasting companies, either. I didn't even try because I was convinced it would be futile. But, of course, years later, I had my own studio and my own nationally syndicated program.

MARSHA: You were—are—fortunate that you didn't know you had to run your whole life according to what other people tell you about this or that profession—that it's too tough, there aren't enough jobs, that it's impossible to qualify, or whatever. All that erroneous information, if we buy it, stops creativity. And it breeds a certain unhealthy dependency on people who have power in those fields. So somehow, as students graduate from school—and I certainly hear this from readers who write letters to me—they have a belief that says, "I need your help to do this thing. I can't do my work without your help or without knowing someone in an influential position." Well, of course, nothing could be further from the truth.

We don't need anyone's help to do our vocation—to come into our own as unique persons. We need to get very good at what we do. We need, say, to have a craft, and if there are dues to be paid in terms of that experience and the expenditure of blood, sweat and tears, we may rightly have to start there—at the ground floor. Many people get their experience through volunteering or apprenticing (for free or very low wages) in the area they want to learn. Certainly esoteric jobs —as in the arts—demand this. I believe in the old adage that says, "If there's a will there's always a way." We don't need spirit-draining connections or huge financial resources but we must develop mastery.

MICHAEL: In your book *Do What You Love, The Money Will Follow* you touched upon resistance and what resistance has to do with not doing what we love.

MARSHA: Right, right. And that goes back to our earlier discussion... that we withhold our own enjoyment; we withhold our own best efforts. When the going gets rough, sometimes instead of confronting the challenge with ardor and our full attention, commitment and tenacity of purpose, we have a tendency to back away. So much of this energy is related to our potential for enjoying life, be it during working hours or leisure time. Resisting, we block our vitality. People who are highly resistant to pleasure don't enjoy anything very much. That's all bound up in the glue of their negativity. Perhaps these become addictive souls. I can certainly see it in my own life when I have to do something I really don't want to do, like preparing for taxes, that being the first example that jumps to my mind. I need great stimulation to get this done. Usually the time-crunch motivates me. That, and the fear of having to pay a penalty for tardy filing!

MICHAEL: I think everyone can appreciate that!

MARSHA: It's not that preparing tax forms is all that difficult. But somehow it's so unpleasant that I postpone it. And my postponing makes the task more difficult. And then I postpone it even more. The cycle worsens. So that's a very simple and common example. Maybe cleaning out the garage would be another case. But resistance is certainly there for some people, not just in these rather odious tasks but in their lives in general. Life itself becomes a noxious task and, in extreme cases, it is almost as if they postpone really living their lives. Resistance can loom very large, indeed, when it comes to doing what we want to do in a job or profession.

Now you might have a wish to write a book or be a sculptor or weed your garden a little more thoroughly, whatever it is. And you suddenly realize that months have gone by and you haven't given yourself that pleasure. So there are decidedly those times when I think we are all resistant, in mysterious ways, blocking ourselves from doing things we really love, which require our own best energies.

MICHAEL: You are saying that sometimes we resist going down that path which would allow us to do what we really love. Why would we do that? Why would we resist the very thing we know could make our lives much fuller and happier?

MARSHA: This gets tricky. There is evidence that most of us are afraid of our own goodness. We're afraid of discovering our best virtue. Afraid of how good we can be. On the most basic level, when we are really talented at something we must give up the myth that we are not capable. We have to give up being irresponsible toward ourselves because being good at something means being competent—that takes much more energy than being incompetent. Then, along with competence comes high, healthy self-esteem, and this often means respecting and taking care of ourselves and others... like the difference between driving an old beat-up junker of a car that you really don't care about and driving a new luxury automobile—say one day getting a Rolls Royce. It's your pride and joy, and you want to keep it in top shape.

That's more work. That's an additional responsibility. You don't just leave it on the street, rusting away.

I also notice that many of us are raised to think of life as this tremendous, harsh struggle. Earlier you spoke of dreams and how many of us simply never allow ourselves to dream about our ideal work. We can't really bring ourselves to believe in our deepest joy—and this is a sad because it's always there; enduring joy is simply a matter of reaching out for it—expectancies—and creating your life that way, in alignment with your dreams.

MICHAEL: It's interesting, you know, talking about dreams. Maybe many of us have a tendency to think of them as being unattainable by their very nature. You know, like they are pure fantasy, storybook stuff. They are not to be taken too seriously. But dreams are much more than this, as you've said.

It strikes me that dreams are the first element in the creative process, even when we're seeking out something as concrete as a job. We talk about creating a mental image of an ideal life and letting that mental picture guide our actions until we have actually manifested in the physical world the thing we've dreamed. In this way, the dream becomes not just a fantasy but a significant power in our lives. What about that line that gets crossed, when dream goes beyond fantasy, becoming a mental image from which a brand new reality is created?

MARSHA: Well you've just said it... that there are people for whom a dream—the vision—is nothing but a fantasy, something that can never come true. This is their rule of life. They don't believe in the possibility of their own vision. And I've never thought of it in exactly this way until I heard you say it—that there are people who do believe in the power of their dreams and use these to create their own realities. This also relates to my research into self-esteem. When we believe we have the power to make our dreams a physical reality, we empower our inner life. That's probably one difference between high and low self-esteem. Sadly, I'm afraid, for the bulk of humankind the best dreams of childhood, or any other dreams for that matter, remain no more than fluff or fantasy, ideas without substance. They never discover their own power in the context of their highest aspirations.

MICHAEL: So where does the feeling of powerlessness come from?

MARSHA: It probably comes from our early experiences of feeling powerless, of never being able to exercise our capacity for impacting other people or the world around us. It may also come from being raised in a situation where you are beaten down and made to feel that you don't have any control of your life. This is abuse in the most poignant sense. Going back to the self-esteem issue, it's such an integral part of doing the work we love. People with healthy self-esteem feel they can make things happen. They feel they can extricate themselves from difficult circumstances, can handle life, and they do feel worthwhile. They feel they are at least okay enough to live a specific way; even when others disapprove of how they live they don't devalue themselves. They think,

"Even if the other person rejects me, it is not sufficient for me to reject myself." In fact, that might even make them more capable of standing in their own corner, being their own best advocate and supporter, that kind of thing. They use their anger or sorrow to fuel their dreams.

MICHAEL: They don't depend on comparing themselves to other people and looking for evidence of how others are inferior.

MARSHA: Not at all. They are self-defining. Returning to the dream issue, the person who is willing to believe that dreams can be actualized as reality is self-defining. Society, teachers, authority figures, the college entrance exams, the professor who says that only two people are going to find a job this year in this field, none of these externals define a person's deepest reality. What defines it is their concrete behavior in the world. They may take small inconsequential steps at first, and then—it's very much like gardening—they plant some tiny seed in the ground. They just water it and care for it and pretty soon a little tiny shoot comes up.

All you have to do in the initial stages of creating the work you love is to view the tiniest of the little shoots coming up. That's feedback from the world that the dream you've put into the play of consciousness is being made manifest. You just need a little positive sprout of feedback to be encouraged.

In my book I write of the potter who began his working life as a teacher. He was a tenured professor and in a very secure position. But he wasn't truly satisfied. He wanted more. He said that for him to leave a tenured profession in which he excelled, and that he liked, was like stepping off a cliff. And yet he really wanted to become a fulltime potter. After many years of thinking about it he took the plunge. Today he is making a good living from his work. He said what kept him going were these little tiny positive feedbacks from the world, the little seed pushing a tiny tendril up through the soil toward the sun. Someone would buy a piece of pottery; he would receive money to continue. He'd win a show; he would get more feedback to continue. Someone would invite him to display in a county fair and so forth. Every one of these was another tendril breaking through the soil and actualizing his dream. And pretty soon he had a full-blown business doing the thing that he most enjoyed.

MICHAEL: Sometimes I think that we expect it to happen magically. You know, it's like the title of your book *Do What You Love, The Money Will Follow*. We think that all we have to do is just sort of start doing what we want to do and by some magic we'll be supported. Is that really the way it works?

MARSHA: No, not quite. As I say in the introduction, it may take a long while for the money to follow. It requires skill, maturity, acumen. It doesn't happen magically. It happens through the most incredible time-consuming efforts for the most part. Now, there are lucky breaks. People do go into a drugstore and get discovered by a movie producer and a week later they are actors or actresses. That's the exception. For most people who wish to make that dream a reality, a lot of hard work and perseverance are involved. And really that's part of the fun of it—the difficulty itself makes the process interesting.

I have a friend who enjoys acting. She has spent years trying to make money at it and now she's starting to—and she recently had the realization that what she really enjoyed was the early years when the challenge was the greatest. She told me, "Show me something that's easy and I'll show you something dull." She enjoys the thing that is difficult... not that everybody does or even should. However, high achievers usually love a challenge—even when they moan about it.

But to get back to your point about magic: When we get too caught up in the magic of it we may undermine our ability and our power to make something happen. Just as it takes a while to grow a tree in the physical universe, so it takes time to grow a business, or whatever it is you want to do. Growth doesn't happen overnight as it does in cartoon-land. Our belief in magic can be yet another way of making sure that we get discouraged and quit before that first living tendril has pushed through the soil toward the light.

MICHAEL: Sometimes you may even have to do something else while you're pursuing what you love.

MARSHA: Right, and it's worth it. Once you are doing what you love doing, it's worth whatever investment of yourself you've made in that thing. I think that to the extent that we invest ourselves—in quality, time, care, love, to say nothing of preventing ourselves from falling victim to our resistance to the enjoyment of life—to the extent we can do all this, we are rewarded. The money will follow. I don't think we can find what we love through another's efforts—such as having a parent open a door of opportunity for us or give us unlimited funds to pursue our interests. All the world's connections may open those doors for you but if you don't invest yourself in the work you're just not going to experience the reward.

MICHAEL: What about all the propaganda we hear where money is concerned—that we must have a lot of it in the bank, that we must make sure to put enough away for our retirement, and so on?

MARSHA: This is such a personal question. Yes, we are taught that we have to save, put away for the future, make certain we have enough in case the economy goes bad and so on. But there are so many people who don't use money that way. All of this has to do with understanding what it means to make choices.

One of the things I stress in my book, and with those with whom I am working, is that we must take responsibility for our choices. Conscious choice means taking responsibility for the ensuing consequences of a choice—positive or negative. So people have differences in terms of what reserves they need. I might think I need $100,000 in the bank to get me through my lean times. Maybe someone else thinks, "I need two years income in the bank before I feel secure." There's nothing wrong with that. Who is it that's judging? Someone else might need much less. I know a woman who earns less than $5,000 a year and she lives beautifully. She lives in a home that she herself handcrafted. She grows her own vegetables. She consumes very, very little. I couldn't live like that. My life is entirely different. We both live responsibly according to the choices we have consciously made.

We often seek formulas, such as these financial recipes you asked about, as a way to avoid doing what we love. We say, "I can't do that because I have to put away money for my retirement, as a cushion for the lean times, and to put my kids through college." You won't hear me say this is wrong. Each of us is unique; this involves money. There's no rule that says you can't wait a couple of years and set yourself up with the specific financial resources you require by saving a few dollars every month, while you study, while you plan with your spouse how he or she might work for a short time while the children are growing up. We needn't jump into that thing we want to do right away, without preparation, without strategic planning or foresight. There are no hard-and-fast laws here. There are no rules saying how much or how little one must have in the bank before starting to do what you love. It's all in what you want to create. It's your choice— including how much money you put in the bank for retirement. This is part of the fun of it—the sheer freedom to play is available.

MICHAEL: You wrote about the three laws of resourcefulness in your book *Do What You Love*. Could you briefly describe what those are?

MARSHA: Sure. Basically I was writing about a person's ability to be resourceful before the money shows up. It might be helpful here to define resourcefulness as creativity—literally, this is the ability to bring something into existence that previously didn't exist, the ability to deal with a variety of situations and challenges and come up with at least adequate solutions. The first law of resourcefulness would be our faith ① FAITH in ourselves, in our ability to solve problems. Here, we know how to use our own brains. ② The second law is independent ② INDEP THINKING thinking, our ability to think autonomously—make difficult decisions alone, even when considerable risk is involved. This includes evaluating risk-effectiveness—what the potential payoff of the risk might be. ③ The third law involves deter- ③ DETER- MINATION mination—the inner persistence or faith we have that says somehow we are going to find a solution to the problem we're facing, even if now we haven't a clue what's to be done.

MICHAEL: So, resourcefulness is being able to tap into our own inner powers, our inner capacities. And I can't help but reflect on how often we inhibit ourselves from doing that. The patterns of our lives can actually prevent us from testing and getting to know those powers. We may be in a hurry, trying to do something that we feel needs to get done, and we don't take the time to stop and search for alternatives, using our own resources. Instead, we grab the quickest and easiest solution. Maybe we calculate that we have to spend six hundred dollars a year to tune up and maintain our car when we could take a class at the local community college and learn how to do it on our own for only fifty dollars a year. Or we think we have to pay a bookkeeper two thousand dollars a year to keep our books, instead of learning an eighty-dollar computer program that would allow us to do it ourselves. I even know people who have never learned to prepare themselves a meal and so they feel they must have enough money to always eat in restaurants. Or, there's the classic case of the woman whose husband dies and she is at a complete loss because he always took care of the finances and she doesn't even know how to balance the checkbook.

MARSHA: Yes. If we turn all our decisions over to the so-called experts, we never get to know our own capabilities. We remain babies. But, as you were talking, it occurred to me that, as discussed, here too we avoid our own power. I keep returning to that because the foundation of doing what we love is knowing (and being willing to grasp the significance of) our own powers. We must know ourselves as people who can express who we truly are, who can live out our deepest inner promptings and actualize our personal gifts. This, as opposed to spending our entire lives never conscious of what we're about, what we're capable of. Most feel so much fear when showing their own power, when exercising it. Women seem especially to have been taught to thwart their power so that the men in their lives won't be threatened, or will approve of them, find them desirable. They maintain the fiction that they are fragile or dependent on men. We are afraid of our own power—men as well as women. I've known men who were so afraid of their own strength that they let themselves be hurt rather than showing strength.

MICHAEL: Years ago I was a visitor at a board meeting for a large non-profit organization. Many of the board members were leading figures in the community. People were arguing and disagreeing and it was all very highly emotional. And at one point this particular person got up and announced that this meeting wasn't fun for him and he really didn't do things that weren't fun. So he was leaving. And everybody just sort of fell silent. The man left and people went back to doing what they were doing before. I learned from this experience that I didn't have to sit through such an agonizing meeting; like the man who left, I could leave. And I did just that. And from that point on, I have always felt I had that choice in virtually any situation.

MARSHA: That's such a wonderful lesson and one that so many of us never learn. For example, we might engage in conversation with someone at dinner and someone will make a remark that we don't agree with or tell a joke that we find offensive. But we'll go along with them as if we agree instead of just sitting quietly, keeping our own counsel. Not that we need to argue outright. There's not always something to be gained by that. But there are many subtle, different ways of stopping a mean remark. And all kinds of words that say, "This is not fun anymore, I'm leaving." There are countless cues that tell another, "Stop, now."

In my practice I find that many managers are terrified of the power within an employee group. They rightly know that at any time employees can come to them, either in a group or alone, and say, "It's not fun around here, we're leaving." Now conversely, employees are terrified that, somehow, managers will hurt them. Everybody is so aware of the other person's power—but all too often suppress their own.

When we have the audacity to say, "This is not fun anymore, I'm leaving;" that's when magical things happen. We feel our own vitality or power. We get in touch with those inner resources that we've forgotten or never even knew we had. It isn't magic, of course. It's our essential depths—reserves of strength. We discover our resources as our power because we have started something. We've planted a seed of self-honesty and the rewards are beginning to sprout.

MICHAEL: So often in large organizations there's an adversarial relationship created between management and the board, between management and employees, or between different departments. The synergy that could develop out of working together doesn't happen and pretty soon the organization can't grow or go forward as it could if that divisiveness wasn't there.

MARSHA: That divisiveness could be neutralized if people talked openly about some of the things we're talking about. The employee or the manager might say, "You know, I've noticed lately our meetings aren't much fun." Just that statement from either party opens doors. People start to talk about it—even enjoy their work a little bit more. But usually we don't do this. We cling to those traditional us-them relationships, and then we notice the negativity grows and grows and that adversarial tone takes over. As a result, a brittleness sets in. Most organizations like this don't last, as our economic journals report.

MICHAEL: In the times that we live in, it has become increasingly difficult for people to think about making it on their own, as a freelancer or an entrepreneurial type. For instance, in the publishing world you hear that for every successful author there are at least a thousand more who are unsuccessful, who can't make a living at it. It's the same for the fine artist or the actor. In the face of such odds, there's a strong tendency to go for security and safety rather than to take any risks. It's not just our concern with money that causes our insecurity; we're also living with the possibility of annihilation through environmental pollution, overpopulation of our planet, and so on, and all this amplifies any anxiety we might be feeling about other things.

MARSHA: Yes, and we must not forget unemployment, deflation and inflation. Everyone worries about these. Yet, ironically, this is a time when the little ordinary guy does have a good chance of making it. Computers, a global economy, new technologies cry to be used, explored. Large organizations are almost at a standstill in terms of being able to respond quickly to change. More and more companies are turning to outside help for many of their services. So I would add that despite how things look, this is a great time to think about what we, as individuals, can offer such companies. The one with the best skills, imagination and quality of service or product will rule!

Going back to our discussion about money in the bank... As I said, different people need different sums of cash. I don't know that there is inherently anything "wrong" with a young person who wants to be a fine artist, for example, first doing whatever he or she must do to gain some sort of financial security. I have no quarrel with that. It's critical to construct the most helpful foundation for our life's work.

In the media today, there's much criticism of the younger generation and their overemphasis on making money. But let's put all that in its proper perspective—that this younger generation is a group of people who will probably have at least two or more major career changes. They may work for five or six years in a row, put money aside in order to build a financial base for themselves and their families. Once that base is established, they can give themselves permission to take a sabbatical, have some freedom to pursue something they truly love. It's almost as if they've reached another stage of their life's education. Instead of earning college credits now they are building their talents, their investments and their life.

I have a client who's only thirty years old, very bright, exceedingly successful. He recently told me, "Marsha, I have something in mind for my later life. This money-making period is just the first leg of a longer journey." This is his time to create many possibilities. People can pursue them all, in a variety of ways—whatever life, money, vocation matches their particular dream, destiny or sense of self, they can move toward this. What a great time to be alive.

MICHAEL: Marsha, one of the things that I got out of reading your book is that you are not necessarily talking about making a lot of money. When you are following your dreams, money itself isn't the pot of gold at the end of the rainbow. For many people, it means making just enough money to support yourself. Sometimes you have to change your lifestyle and turn your life in a new direction, to maybe make less money but actually improve your life in the process.

MARSHA: As you say this, a story comes to mind about a friend of mine; this young man was a graduate student in English. When he found out how much research he was going to have to do, and noticed the rigors of publishing and so on, he thought it over and came to the conclusion that he really didn't want to have an academic career. Instead of going for a secure college teaching job, he went into carpentry. He began in the late '60s working for about $3.50 an hour.

Today he is making an excellent living. The thing that impressed me about his decision was his emphasis on wanting to take control of his life. Now, no one tells him how he's going to make a building. He runs his own show. He is discriminating about the kinds of people he works for.

Let me give you another example. I know a young architectural student who, around the age of twenty-five, decided he would open his own firm rather than taking a job with a large company. Right after graduating from college he started his own business. You must understand that it takes many years to build such a business. Doing what he did means he had some very lean years, at least five or six.

Now this is a young man who loves to go out to dinner. He's very social. He loves nice clothes, fancy cars and all the rest. But for the time being he lives in a one-room flat. He says sometimes he has hot water, sometimes not. He doesn't entertain or travel or go out to dinner. He's putting all of his energy into his practice, keeping his focus on designing and building only beautiful buildings.

He's an excellent example of how we might need to give something up, in terms of immediate rewards, in order to build our dream. I know this individual quite well and I am certain that in a few years he will be hugely successful. He'll be well able to enjoy those dinners out and gorgeous clothes and all the rest. But for the short term, his life is Spartan, to say the least. So that's one kind of judgment-call we might make in order to eventually be able to do what we love.

MICHAEL: And that, of course, brings up the whole subject of the role of money and doing what you love.

MARSHA: Not everybody wants or requires a lot of money, of course. This is easy to overlook in our society, where the amount of money we have is perceived as a measure of our success. Some people are quite sufficiently joyful focusing their attention fully on the thing that they love to do. Like the potter who says that he knows there's a little piece of himself in every item he makes. It gives him great pleasure to shape the pot with his hands and his mind and also to think of that little piece of himself entering the lives of the people who purchase that pot and bring it into their homes. That's enough for him. He doesn't require a lot of money or the things money can buy. He measures his success and his wealth in a very different way.

Sometimes it seems that we need large salaries as compensation for the alienation we feel when we do work that we don't like. So maybe there's a sliding scale there—we can do with a lot less money if we're fulfilled in other ways. That's such an individual thing. Each of us has our own special list of requirements for living out our dreams.

MICHAEL: So, you're advising us that we should perhaps be cautious about equating money and success.

MARSHA: More than that, we each need to take responsibility for defining success in our own terms. For me, having a healthy level of vitality is the measure of a successful life. Look at people's vitality levels. If their way of life is deadening instead of invigorating them, what good will all the money in the world be?

Workaholics can claim to be happy with their work but whether they are or not will be revealed in their robustness, their vitality. You can't lie about that; vigor, enthusiasm shows through regardless of how we may try to fool ourselves. Vitality is what distinguishes the person who loves his or her work passionately from the person who is a workaholic.

Sometimes it's difficult to tell the difference between a workaholic and the person who is so much in love with what they do that they can barely stand to leave it. Picasso, for example, was feverishly involved in his work—he was at it day and night. It was the center of his life. Everything else came second. Was he a workaholic? Not in my book. The workaholic works to stave off fear and anxiety; those who love their work can play, can go to the park, to the beach, lie in a hammock and just stare at the sky. But they love their work. It's part of who they are, their aliveness, fulfillment, love. In the workaholic, work itself is full of anxiety. Though it may not always look that way to an outsider, there is no real love in the work. It's only a means to an end, with the end being avoidance of pain, alienation, perhaps suppressed rage.

"I need more money," the workaholic might typically say; "I need more approval; what will they say if I make a mistake?" These are some of the motivations that ruthlessly drive workaholics. On the face of it you can't always tell the difference between someone who is a workaholic and someone who loves their work. Be assured, however, that appearances are deceiving. And really that's not our concern unless the person happens to be a close family member. Our concern ought to be just with ourselves.

MICHAEL: In your writing you speak of love and work, and of how as we learn to love we also learn to demand love in our work. Could we go into that a bit?

MARSHA: Yes. We are what we love. We are love and so everything we do is touched by its presence or absence. When I work around someone who is doing work they love, I become aware of what I call their "heat." It's love; their personal passion or intensity is not born of anger and anxiety. It's born of love. There's no other word for it. It's just Creation working through them.

▲
Section Two
▼

Whole Living:
Creative Choices

The life we experience is closely related to the choices we make on a day-to-day basis. How we choose to live today creates the future we will experience tomorrow. For this reason, if no other, the best choices we can make are those that come from the deepest parts of ourselves. These are the choices that most closely reflect who we really are, helping us to actualize our greatest potential. Paradoxically as we work more deeply with our inner lives, and are able to make choices that honor our true nature, the more the outer world seems transformed, supporting our efforts to express our greatest gifts and actualize our fondest dreams.

When we make choices that fail to honor who we really are—say when we are trying to please other people or when we are trying to avoid making waves—we are in danger of becoming alienated from ourselves. Even not choosing is a choice. And that choice can have just as much impact as any other on the world we experience. As we learn to be more aware of our choices and how they affect our lives, we discover that every choice is a marker on a path to greater self-esteem, self-respect, and self-realization. For this reason we have much to gain by looking more closely at how we make choices and how our choices affect us.

• • •

MICHAEL: Marsha, one of the things you discuss in your book *Elegant Choices, Healing Choices* is that it is important to become more conscious of the details of our lives. You say that in your own life you have become increasingly aware that details count, that even the seemingly minor choices we make can either lower or elevate the life we experience. Isn't this another way of saying that it all adds up to being who we are, that the small decisions as well as the big ones matter?

MARSHA: Yes, exactly. In the long run every choice we make contributes to who we are or who we are becoming. It could be that at the moment we make a choice it doesn't have a big impact on us, or doesn't seem to.

Imagine this, that in our minds we have a camera and a tape recorder. These are always "on," recording what we are doing and what we are experiencing throughout our lives. With this inner camera we are always taking snapshots and with the recorder we are always recording what we hear ourselves saying to and about ourselves. If you add that up over the years, you begin to get a very consistent picture, or series of pictures—like an inner scrapbook of all life's experiences. That image pretty clearly reveals what you're about.

I should add that my research and professional work is predominantly with healthy, self-actualizing adults. What I see in this group is that their "snapshot collection" is largely self-respecting and self-affirming. When they look at their mental snapshots they seem to say, "Oh, I'm the kind of person who values such and such. I'm the kind of person who takes proper care and time, who tries to make certain that everything I do is done well, who takes great pleasure in a job well done."

Each choice made by the emotionally healthy, self-actualizing person seems to flow easily, flexibly, with the person receiving a sort of guidance from these inner pictures. They trust their own guidance above external judgments or cliches that may strongly influence the choices of people who are less self-actualized.

There's also a certain symmetry or aesthetic consistency between their choices and these inner pictures. This can be quite elegant. You and I are going to have different inner snapshots or internal "recordings." But there will be an aesthetic consistency or an integrity there (what I call elegance) that we'll probably find exciting and pleasing even if we have very different opinions or values. It's like looking at a great work of art: We may not enjoy the same specific imagery but if we grasp the artistic integrity of the whole artwork we'll be moved by its basic elegance.

MICHAEL: You use the term "self-actualizing person." Could you describe what that is?

MARSHA: The self-actualizing person is, by definition, a highly individualized, whole and creative person, generally spontaneous, in the sense of trusting their own choices in the ways we've begun to discuss here. They are people who are "coming into their own"—as whole persons, efficient and authentic in the areas of life-choices and values. They tend to be less fearful, more self-accepting than people whose fears and self-doubts block them from making truthful choices or taking action in life.

Abraham Maslow pointed out that so-called "well adjusted" persons often reject much of their own depths or humanity. To be well adjusted in society's terms, Maslow claimed, there had to be a splitting of the person, where we turn our backs on who we really are. We pay a significant price when we do this, since we squander depths that are the source of our ability to play, to love, to experience joy, to laugh and, most importantly, to create. Maslow used a wonderful phrase to describe the opposite of the self-actualizing process: by protecting ourselves against the hell within us, we also cut ourselves off from the heaven within.

MICHAEL: Then you're suggesting that the self-actualizing person is one who is emotionally healthy to the extent that they are capable of making good choices—good choices according to the idea of embracing their true nature.

MARSHA: Yes. Maslow, who some thirty years ago was a leading pioneer in this field, wrote that if we tell self-actualized people to choose what they will, it will usually turn out okay. But if we tell the person who is not tending toward emotional health to choose what they will, we have no guarantee that their choice will turn out to be okay. That person's choices could take him or her anywhere and might have nothing to do with health, or their true self. They could just as easily shoot themselves in the foot or compulsively repeat a toxic and self-defeating habit.

In my work, I have been so fortunate to know people who are tending toward self-actualization. I also find that this same group is willing and skillful when looking at how they make choices. And what I find is that, indeed, their choices are self-affirming, are life-supporting. They have what Maslow called the "Being values," including beauty, simplicity, self-sufficiency, aliveness, uniqueness, joy, humor, playfulness, honesty, the ability to find unity in apparent opposites, a personal aesthetic, courage and so on. This is not to say that every single choice they make is a "good" one; however, over time their choices add up to a kind of elegance. What's more, they feel the presence of these healthy patterns in their lives and know they can count on their own tendency to make further choices that serve them well.

[margin note: Being value]

MICHAEL: It seems to me that when we look at choices we often think of them in terms of the outer world, or external events and decisions—like what kind of car to buy or where we're going to go for our summer vacation. We less commonly think of choices in terms of our inner life, that we can choose how we are going to experience an event. This seems particularly to be the case when there is an event that is difficult, one we would prefer not to have to face.

For instance, let's say we must attend the funeral of a loved one, or that we are going to be spending a lot of time with someone who is seriously ill. These are experiences that we may not feel we have a choice about. We have to do them. Life somehow requires it. The only area of choice open to us is how we experience it, not the experience itself. Do you think we have the ability to choose how we experience our lives, as distinct from what we experience?

MARSHA: It's certainly true that we have a choice about how we are going to approach a particular event and also a choice about how we are going to experience it. Let's take the example you mention, of having to attend a friend's funeral or caring for a loved one who is very ill. It can be helpful at such times to ask ourselves, "How would it be if I were willing or entirely open to doing this?" If we wrestle with this question honestly and openly, we'll begin to discover that we do have choices about how we experience these events. And the inherent possibility of having many other such choices can transform us—shows us the potential of life.

First of all, we may have this awareness, "Oh my goodness, life could be totally different than it is. My modus operandi could be totally different. My body language, my emotional state, my eye contact, my physical expression, my face and so forth, could all be altered if I chose differently." So that question alone begins to address how we make a choice. The external event isn't changed in and of itself. But the inner dynamic can change dramatically.

You know, in the opening of *Elegant Choices, Healing Choices,* I cite a poem by Walt Whitman, who talks of how we misrepresent ourselves most of our lives. We present to the world a self that is difficult to respect and love. But he suggests that we are truly organs of the soul and when we let the soul appear through our actions, it—and these are his words—makes our knees bend. Well, I experience this as true. We can choose with that part of ourselves that is stunningly virtuous. Once we understand this, we truly have a choice.

St. Augustine wrote that the "good" person is in love with his or her own good will. It pleases him or her to be willing to be open to whatever his or her fundamental decency is. It pleases her to be willing to be in that relationship with the sick relative, let's say. It pleases him to be a decent individual. When we begin to enjoy our own goodness, our own fundamental decency, our willingness revolutionizes our approach to life from moment to moment and day to day. It's really amazing and so simple... a healing choice that brings us closer to our own wholeness.

MICHAEL: I think our tendency is so often just the opposite. We relate only to that part Whitman says we can't respect. We can be pretty hard on ourselves, and get down on ourselves because of our own resistance to these difficult situations, and that can sometimes compound the problem of doing what you're suggesting.

MARSHA: Again, we come back to the real purpose of becoming more conscious in our lives, the ultimate purpose being to discover our wholeness, which must include acceptance of our essential goodness. You know, Michael, over the years you have interviewed a number of spiritual leaders, Buddhist monks, great spiritual teachers, and people who devotedly practice meditation. What we're discussing here —choices and conscious living—is closely related to a spiritual practice. Making choices of the kind we're discussing can be viewed in the same context as any spiritual discipline except that it offers us an ordinary "waking" process.

If we can just get quiet and calm enough we enter that stillness that is not part of our self-critical, self-deprecating, outer persona. Here, we find kindness and gentleness, good will—not just toward others but toward ourselves. Every healthy, fully-functioning, self-actualizing person knows and accepts the fact that they are both weak and strong, powerful yet also vulnerable and defenceless, innocent yet tarnished, ordinary and also special. As we go within, and quiet ourselves, as the contemplatives do, we touch that life-giving spirit which does not fear or judge. It is from this life-impulse that we learn to relate to what Whitman calls the soul.

We're hard on ourselves only because we have not yet learned that we can choose in the direction of our essential goodness, that it is already there to be chosen. The self-judgment and discounting of ourselves is our learned habit, something we began very early in life, probably when we were infants. Then, we haven't yet realized that we have other choices. When we can be kind and gentle toward ourselves, when we quiet our harsh, critical and fearful voice—just silence it a little bit—we begin to establish a relationship with the life-spirit. We see that this sweet way of being is a choice.

MICHAEL: Your suggestion about asking yourself what you would do if you were really willing to be there, no matter how difficult the situation, reminds me of another hypothetical question. This one is a little different but I think it brings us to another question about choices. To do this we imagine that we have chosen our parents, or our brother, or our sister,

Soul

or perhaps a person who seems to be very difficult for us to deal with. Then we ask ourselves, why did we choose them? *Why?* By doing this, we suddenly get a very different perspective on life. We become aware of a different set of choices—or at the very least we begin to see that we really do have choices.

MARSHA: Right. It's these sorts of questions that make us more aware of what it means to be human. But I am also reminded here that we can become too introspective, you know. The point here is not to withdraw or probe around, endlessly psychologizing, on every choice—like should I use salt and pepper or just salt or just pepper? Rather, I'm speaking in broader, universal terms, of generally awakening to the nature of our choices and what these mean to us in the larger picture or symmetry of life.

Maslow's point was that if we wish to be fully self-actualizing, we must look within at our hell as well as our heaven. To do that we need to learn how to be kind to ourselves, *Kind.* to show our fundamental kindness to ourselves. To ask questions like the ones you pose about why we have chosen to have certain people in our lives, lets us assume responsibility for our lives. These questions remind us that we are the ones who are snapping those mental pictures. We're the ones who are creating and listening to the inner narrative about our life experience.

Ultimately the world benefits from our healthy choices. There develops a sweetness in people who are able to be gentle toward themselves. Remember the ancients who said that *Soul breathe* when we let the soul breathe through our intellect it is genius. When we let the soul breathe through our will it is

virtue. And when we let it flow through our affections, it is
love.

Choosing these ideas, we cease judging ourselves harsh-
ly. And when we are generous and kind toward ourselves it
naturally follows that we become more generous and kindly
toward our sisters and brothers; and the more generous we
are with our brothers and sisters the more generous they'll be
with us. So our willingness to examine our inner hell with
receptive kindness has a positive effect on the entire world.
And it all starts with just a simple question—how am I
speaking to myself? Would I speak to a beloved child this
way? A child that I adore? Usually, we speak more kindly to
a child we love than we do to ourselves.

MICHAEL: Marsha, here's a question that often arises in my
interviews in some form or another: Is it possible to choose
happiness?

MARSHA: Well, yes and no. We can choose to be happy by
accepting whatever comes up in our lives, by welcoming
rather than resisting what the world places before us. And
we can be happy by forgetting the quest for happiness and
courting its richer cousin—joy. The joyful person is vital,
involved, finds satisfaction in work or relationships or just
puttering around the house or feeding the birds... in short,
they don't think so much about what will—materially or sit-
uationally—make them happy. In effect, they just do it. We
spend far too much time looking for happiness. Like, "Gee, I
wish I could find a job that would make me happy!" Or, "I
wonder if a relationship with this person will do it?" Or, "If I

could only write a bestselling book or lose ten pounds, or spend next summer in Hawaii, then I'd be happy."

Happiness isn't a destination; it's part of a process. Happiness seems to come to people when they are not paying attention to it one way or another.

MICHAEL: Well, maybe it's coming to them because they're paying attention to the here and now, to the moment. *To the moment*

MARSHA: To the moment, yes. That's where happiness is, and the minute you cut that connection with the moment, you cut your opportunity for experiencing joy... which, of course, means that happiness slips by you, too.

MICHAEL: My experience has been that our ability to choose and to be in the moment is directly related to our pre-occupation with the past or the future or with what we are doing or have just done. The baseball player who starts thinking too much about the fact that the bases are loaded and he's got two strikes against him is probably going to lose it and strike out...

MARSHA: That's right. And it's important to realize that we can choose to be more fully present. But if you are worrying or fearful, your emotions and thoughts throw you off. You start wrestling with phantoms and what the Bible calls principalities of darkness—and these are really very powerful controlling factors. "Should I? Shouldn't I?" "Am I right or wrong?" But if you are truly living in the moment you're liberated, you're innocent. You can choose freely.

MICHAEL: In your book you talked about the Adam and Eve myth and how it represents an archetypal myth that explains how we got to this point of not being able to be in the moment. Can you say something about the choices involved in this myth?

MARSHA: Well, the Tree of Knowledge holds the fruits of good and evil. And Adam and Eve were warned against partaking of it. In this analogy, we find good and evil are the foundation of duality, that is, our experience of separation, of being out of touch with the Garden of Eden, where life is lived totally in the present. Separation first happened when humans tried to be like God, not realizing that in their faith in God they already had it all. The story of Adam and Eve teaches us that prior to our knowledge of good and evil, we all stand on holy ground. But one little bite of the apple from the Tree started us erroneously thinking about good and evil, past, present and future, and all the worrying, and suddenly we are out of touch with the holy present. Through our own disobedience and preoccupation with these matters, we are banished from the Garden of Eden. This separation is the essence of sin.

MICHAEL: It's interesting to note that the word "sin" comes from the Greek word that means "missing the mark," or "being off the path."

MARSHA: That certainly fits, doesn't it?

MICHAEL: The word "separation" as you use it here seems to imply that there is a relationship, that is, between ourselves and others or between ourselves and a higher power, or God.

MARSHA: Yes. One of the questions we might ask ourselves when we feel resistant is, "Am I avoiding relationship?" There are many ways of being in relationship. There's the relationship with another person—intimacy when it's at its best. And I'm speaking not of sexual intimacy so much as the nature of the sealed connection. Intimacy can also apply to our connection or relationship with the moment. "Am I avoiding relationship with the here-and-now?" Very often, when I'm avoiding something that's difficult, that I don't care to do, I'll ask myself this question, "Am I avoiding relationship?" Sure enough it often turns out that I am. It's helpful to have a way of reminding ourselves.

MICHAEL: So this kind of reminder can help us enter into the relationship?

MARSHA: For me it does. Just a gentle reminder of such questions reminds me that I have a choice. And I believe that whenever the question even occurs to us it indicates that we are wanting to feel more connected, less separated.

MICHAEL: You speak of our knowledge of good and evil being at the center of our feelings of separation, or sin, missing the mark… It would almost seem then that the greater our knowledge, in that respect, the more difficult it would be for us to choose, to make what you call elegant choices.

MARSHA: Durkheim once wrote that in a community of saints, the least transgression would be a terrible sin. Sometimes I observe our human community and think how hard we are on ourselves... that we, too, get preoccupied with our smallest transgressions. We need to remember that the more we appreciate our potential for goodness, the more good we can be. Now we don't want to overdo this. But again I remind us all that there is in all of us something virtuous, someone virtuous, the "inner person of the heart." Let us honor that. You know, that's really important, to choose each moment to honor the one inside who is pure and virtuous. And in time, as we choose to honor that one, our lives reflect that virtue. I believe what we really want is to live our virtue. Virtue is not just a particular trait, it's a condition of mind and heart and intention, just the basic sweetness we see in people.

MICHAEL: In your book you told about the woman who reached a point in her life where she said she didn't make decisions anymore, that it was just a continuum of life moving through her. There wasn't a place where she decided to do this or that.

MARSHA: That's one of my examples of a healthy chooser. She happens to be a sculptor who has been creative all of her life. She responds to her moments fully, appropriately. For example, she speaks of her grandchildren visiting her and wanting her to go with them on a picnic. At that instant she preferred to be writing a poem, haiku. She thought to herself, "Now what would I prefer to do now, this very moment? What is my natural inclination now?" She chose to stay home to write poetry and sent the children off, on their own, to have their picnic. She describes how from that choice other choices flow. She could choose to write more poetry or have more quiet time for herself. That kind of flow is important to honor. Instead we more often get caught up in thoughts like "How should I be with my grandchildren now," and "I should go on the picnic with them because it's such a nice day today"... you know, we are listening to our intellect instead of the more organic, spontaneous aspect of self.

MICHAEL: Well, I think there's something in our culture that demeans the instinctual or the feeling level, an attitude that if it can't be analyzed and investigated scientifically, and understood rationally, then it's not real. Certainly in our educational system we are told not to trust that part of ourselves.

MARSHA: That is the fruit of good and evil again. We dissect everything intellectually, again and again. I am not anti-intellectual. But let's put the intellect in its proper place. Everything ought not to be driven by logic. This is an analytical, harsh function. Let our mind serve the softer parts of self—the heart and soul—for a change. In education we cut ourselves off, suppress, repress, and deny all the soft feeling parts of our lives. We even carry this mechanism over into family relationships. I see this when people ask me for a formula or a prescription for their lives... that's part of this overemphasis on the rational side. We are not machines. Let's flow a bit with ourselves, and let this happen easily. Instead, people want a formula, a blueprint. It's a tough call to tell people when to stop being overly analytical and flow with it. This is not something another person can prescribe for us. That's one of the requirements for growing up, that we are often alone in figuring out how to flow, to love, to live.

MICHAEL: So it's a matter of balance, paying attention to the instinctual as well as the intellect.

MARSHA: Yes. That's why I write that we have to let intellect play its part, as it was meant to do, and not go too far either way. Recognizing this, too, is our choice. Be balanced. Take time to meditate, pray, contemplate. Look at the results you're getting from that. A human being knows whether something is helpful, appealing or not—whether something is productive or not, whether it is fatiguing or not, toxic or not and so on.

Part of our adult development is learning to discern and then respect what we know. Learn to be a better discerner. Perhaps become more independent of the expert and the authority figures in our lives. The rigid person swallows, or implodes, the authority. Then free choice becomes impossible for them.

MICHAEL: Historically, do you think we have more choices now or fewer? Do you think the ability to choose stays constant pretty much throughout history?

MARSHA: Well, I think today we have more options, more opportunities for choosing. That's probably why it seems like our choices are more limited; it's almost overwhelming. Let me give you an example. I work with corporations that are undergoing a lot of change, mergers, "downsizing" and so on. Usually only the most progressive companies ask me to work with them. And those companies are actually very permissive. They give their employees a lot of room to be creative, innovative. In fact, sometimes my assignment is to encourage people, to help guide them toward their own bold innovations.

I notice that many people don't believe these encouragements and permissions are real. They don't know if management can be trusted. Yet within the scope of their eight-hour day there is plenty of time for creative projects. Only the most creative, autonomous workers take advantage of these permissions or know what to do with freedom.

Our options are enormous today. We live longer. We have the opportunity to live where we want to live. We don't have a caste system. We don't have to follow in our parents' footsteps. We can marry whom we want. We don't even have to marry. We don't have gender roles given to us in the same fashion, and we don't belong to people anymore as when half the women in the world were chattel, considered the property of their fathers. The fathers could give them away—sell them—to whomever they wanted. So, I'd say we have many options if we are just willing to take off our blindfolds. But we don't want to do this because it means accepting tremendous responsibility. If I choose to take off my blindfold, I am stuck with the consequences of that choice and that's frightening. You know, stunningly lavish options—it's that kind of thing.

MICHAEL: That brings me to my next question, that sometimes we don't make choices simply because we don't want the responsibility.

MARSHA: I would agree. And yet, my own experience, both personally and professionally, has been that the more willing we are to make those hard choices and take responsibility for them, the more we really live. Somehow, the energy we get by making a small choice can be quite extraordinary. You spoke earlier about a funeral... well, let's suppose that a parent has just died. Maybe it is a parent who has abused us in some way. It may have been physical abuse or emotional abuse... there are all kinds of dysfunctional family situations where a person might feel angry or resentful toward that parent. So let's say the adult child is now faced with a choice of going to that funeral and perhaps resolving the old conflict. Now, you have at least two choices. You can decide not to go because you simply don't like that person. You could entertain all kinds of rationalizations for not going, such as the fact that in childhood they hurt you or they were never supportive of you or whatever. Or, you can choose to go and accept whatever might happen in the process. The minute you choose to go, all the energy that was bottled up with your memories of that person begins to be released. It's like when an acupuncture needle pierces the spot where your pain is, and the pain melts away. When we are willing to be responsible for our pain, it's as if we are then willing to be healed. We're accepting our life's consequences, saying, "This is what my life is authentically about, and this is who I am. I'll live with it and take the risk of being totally real. I'll let go of fear and make the choices that help heal me and others."

MICHAEL: So often, we hold ourselves back because we're afraid of what people will say or what they will think.

MARSHA: We fear what people will say, what people will think. But that's not all. We cling to the dreams of our childhood. When we idealized how our lives would be, when we had fairy-tale pictures of how life was going to turn out. When we finally choose to say, "I might not get that dream," when we're willing to let that dream go, we get something better: our real life. Usually I find that when I am at last willing to be responsible for my fears, own them, and stop imposing my fantasy on life, life reveals itself to me. Life begins to unfold in a fresh way, a novel, surprising way. Both Nietzsche and Kazantzakis spoke about having the courage to be who we are. This courage to be who we are is tremendously invigorating and energizing. It is from this zest that life begins to work, to flow, to unfold.

MICHAEL: Your mention of Kazantzakis reminds me of Zorba the Greek. Zorba was this poor peasant man who had a tremendous zest for life. His energy and his expressions of life were energizing for others and he inspired other people with his own life… He chose life and was able to be responsible for who he was, regardless of dreams that had been destroyed or fears, and it was out of these choices that his zest and energy came.

MARSHA: You know, that's another kind of choice we can make. We can ask, "What inspires me? Who inspires me?" We can look around at fictional characters like Zorba, or real-life characters, maybe someone we admire in our family or circle of friends, perhaps a political figure. We could find that they inspire us and give us models of how to make those difficult choices and let us be more open to life.

MICHAEL: Where are they? Where are these heros that might inspire us?

MARSHA: We all have different heros, of course. We can find ours through our continual self-questioning. It's the questioning, "What inspires me? Who inspires me? What would I have to do to inspire myself?" Now that's a great inquiry! I mean you could take these questions and roll them around your mind during a weekend retreat. Or you might, you know, ask yourself these questions while you were doing nothing special, like the Buddhists' saying, "chop wood and carry water"—clean your house, clean out the garage. Just keep running the inquiry through your mind and don't talk too much, no socializing. Just ask, "What would I have to do to inspire myself?" Those large questions can move us a long way in our personal growth, if we're honest. They can remind us that even being willing to be inspired is a choice.

MICHAEL: You know, when you mention the silence, being quiet, and coming to a choice, I am reminded of how often we choose to distract ourselves. We actually choose distractions. We choose to watch television instead of going outside. Or we choose to go off on some adventure that is going to take us away from our family. We choose distractions.

MARSHA: Yes. We choose to cut the connection with the holy present. I once had a meditation teacher who told me that only a strong person can really meditate because the silence of the present is so overpowering. It's not so much that the silence does anything to us but in our silence we meet ourselves. This is a powerful experience. So we have to prepare. To take a little bit of silence at a time is probably the best way. If a person can't sit for an hour, maybe they can sit for five minutes. Take silence a little at a time.

You know, Michael, for the last twenty or twenty-five years I've been examining adult growth and development. At the uppermost levels of that development I find a strong spiritual component. Often, at the beginning stages, we are motivated more by some of the things that a youthful person would be motivated by—stimulation and excitement or obliterating our flaws or analyzing our early lives. We may court adventure and conquest or whatever. That's not to say there's anything wrong with this. But later on in our lives, after a period of discovery as we know ourselves a little better, our spiritual dimension starts to emerge. When that happens we begin to seek out experiences that develop these faculties further—listening to music or walking or meditating or writing in a journal, painting or prayer... any number of things that honor this deepest growth in ourselves. It's all part of a developmental picture.

MICHAEL: When you say developmental picture you mean like stages or cycles?

MARSHA: More stages than cycles. A cycle implies a circle, something fixed and tidy that keeps repeating. For me, stages suggest evolution, a going-forward rather than a circling around. A stage seems to me to be part of a natural progression, a movement that continues with or without a crisis or experts or someone else's help... it just happens naturally because it is part of an organic movement, like birth, puberty, old age, death. I recently saw a greeting card for new parents, expressing something to the effect that a baby was God's way of saying the world will continue. It's like that; this happens, so you might as well relax. The more we relax about these stages the more movement happens. The quicker we will develop, really. When we try to force it or resist it, it's counter-productive.

MICHAEL: I think it is true in the west more than in the east, that we live as if change and transformation are related to crisis. We feel there must be a crisis. We must come to some point of being forced to confront something in ourselves or in our external world. And really, transformation can occur without our coming to that.

MARSHA: Exactly, this is so true. Again we interpret change and transformation as natural, and simply allow them to happen. Sometimes this seems the most radical statement one can make, and one that people resist and protest. The truth is that transformation occurs when we take it easy, let go of struggle, when we are willing to let things happen. We can direct what happens, certainly, but we don't need so much effort. Our clinging effort is just another distraction.

I sense that aggressive action gets in our way. We are taught that we must be very aggressively active... there's fear about life involved here. I was talking earlier with a young man, perhaps twenty years old. He was just out of college and he was debating with me. His argument was that you had to be active or you can't get this or that done in your career. And I was thinking, "It will probably happen anyway, so you can just relax about it." The mystery of life, how it unfolds, how it is going to be regardless of our efforts...

that's something that few appreciate until they're ready to appreciate it. Then it's a marvel—awe, wonder.

MICHAEL: It reminds me of something Joseph Campbell said, that his only regret was not really appreciating certain fleeting moments with people... grasping the importance of that moment only when he looked back and, maybe from the broader perspective or fuller understanding that had come in the interim, he realized how important that moment had been with this person. I look back over my life and notice there were people in my life that were very pivotal, very important. Yet they had only a very small place in my life in terms of time we were together. I remember them and say to myself, I got so much, yet if I'd only paid more attention; if I'd only been more in the moment with them!

MARSHA: Yes, it's intimacy, really, relationship, silence, mystery, love... this love is so powerful. Mother Theresa once commented that this love always hurts. That quality may be what Joseph Campbell was talking about. When we are gentler with ourselves and others, when we are more present, there's always a bit of pain in there, because there is such profound richness in life when we are not distracting ourselves or trying to avoid it. Do you know what I mean? In a perverse sort of way, it's easier to distract ourselves with television, or by getting into the car and driving our brains out to get to a place we didn't want to go in the first place... it's easier to do that than to sit with a friend or relative with whom we've had some problems and work it out and embrace them and then realize that it's all been handled and we really love each other. That's pain because we wasted so

much time holding onto the old problem and distracting ourselves from relationship. That kind of pain—or poignancy—
is very real.

MICHAEL: There does seem to be in most of us a need to be
noticed, to make our mark in the world. We need to achieve
something, be recognized. And there's another piece, which
you have already suggested, that also wants the silence,
wants the quiet. So there's this conflict between wanting to
be noticed and wanting to be silent.

MARSHA: Well, again the developmental framework seems
to answer some of that, at least for me. Think of an adolescent: The adolescent has a strong need to impose his or her
personality on the family and community. The ego needs are
very intense and developing strong self-esteem is important.
It's right that this should happen. It's the achievement and
adventure stage I have spoken about; it's right and proper.
As it says in Ecclesiastes, "To everything there is a season.
There is a time for every purpose under the sun." So I don't
suggest we do life any other way. For most of us there is this
natural desire to make our mark in the world and then the
desire to be silent. We don't choose one or the other; we do
both. To a person who has the desire to achieve, I say, go for
it, honor it, go. Just don't be surprised if one day a little voice
inside you says, "Okay, you did that, now I want you to pay
attention to the next thing and this next thing is completely
different." You know, the Book of Isaiah says, "Behold I will
do a new thing." You know, the Lord is speaking, and says,
"Behold I will do a new thing," and "Think not of former
things." Okay, then, in each of us there comes a time when

we feel an impulse that says, "Okay, time for a brand new thing, folks; time to stop remembering former things." So then we let go. Or try to. Maybe it's so threatening that we resist. That too is natural, our resistance—our feeling of great vulnerability. We need to learn how to lighten up—to make it okay, make it all right to move slowly, as a child might. Keep accepting whatever surfaces: I see it, I accept it, I resist not... I fold it all into that omelette of life, you know. At the upper mature levels of development we appreciate all this mystery—silence, love, intimacy, all these things for their special contribution. These let us live in a way that there is no separation, no difference between us and the other.

Aristotle wrote that a friend is another self. For me, my readers are "other selves." You're another self. If I'm in the present moment, you're truly another self, Michael. Now if I am intellectualizing, psychologizing, stressed out, doing all these distracting things, I'm the only self. But the minute I enter this connection here, right here, intimately in the middle where our two spirits are dancing around the room together, there is no barrier between me and you. It's I and Thou. We're in a place where we can just let ourselves be— and be present. I'm basically saying, "There's not much else to do folks, just relax and enjoy the ride and give something back in the process." Which we do anyway when we enjoy life's ride because the energy is so lush, so charming in those realms, so warm.

MICHAEL: Well, I hear the protests, "That's all well and good for you but what about me? My life is very different. I can't do that."

MARSHA: Well, if you can't do that then don't do that. Do whatever you can do. Honor and live in the light you have. We can only do that anyway. There is really no alternative but to live the light you have, in the best way you can. To the person who says, "I can't do that," my only reply is to say, "You have something you want, something that's important to you. You have a best self, some fundamental essential goodness, and wherever you are right now, the ground you stand on is holy ground. So stand there and be beautiful, wherever you are. I'll do my life and you do yours."

MICHAEL: Yes, I like that… that really we can choose to see the beauty in ourselves.

MARSHA: Thomas Merton said such a beautiful thing: He was talking about adult maturity, spiritual maturity especially… he was talking about the beginning of this maturity as a time when we realize that we are good at some things and limited at some things and that others will be competent at the very things we are limited in. So we find this fit between us and others. Together we are a spiritual whole; alone we are only parts of the whole. Growing up, becoming spiritually mature, means we'll recognize that we are not the center of the universe, that we're all part of the same universe; we're interrelated parts. I need you and you need me to be truly secure. So one person says, "That's not for me." We can say to that person, "Someone needs you and you need someone else." If you do nothing else but simply accept that you are needed for the things that you do, you begin to feel secure, at least in that. That's a comfort. Because many people don't feel that they are good for anything, they don't even try to make a contribution. Then we all suffer.

MICHAEL: Really, in some sense we're all here to make a contribution and we can only do that as we allow our true selves to emerge.

MARSHA: Yes. It's like you will deprive the other of your essential goodness, your virtue, your talent, your effort, your relationship, your humor, your beauty if you don't believe you have it to give. So our first job is to cultivate these elements in ourselves. It may sound selfish at first, but it's not. On the contrary! Again we return to that organic image of a tree: The baby fruit tree has to take from the soil first; then, later, it gives back delicious fruit.

MICHAEL: It's a fascinating paradox, isn't it, that as we go inside the outside changes. And the reverse also seems to be true. There's a John Muir quote that I like very much. He said that when he went outside he found he was going in.

MARSHA: That's beautiful. Perhaps spiritual maturity is our realization that, indeed, we are living in an interactive universe, one that we help to create through what we ourselves contribute by our presence here. We may be taught to think of the world as fixed and finite but the choices we make, even those we make only in consciousness, softly influence the whole. In this respect, for good or bad, our choices are always creative choices. Realizing this, we acknowledge the creative power we each possess. Remember this is ongoing—a minute-to-minute, daily phenomenon: As Scripture teaches—"Choose ye this day whom ye will serve." That, perhaps, is the essence of whole living and creative choices.

▲

Section Three

▼

Making Fairy Tales Come True

MICHAEL: Everyone wants to be happy, and the search for happiness is universal. At the same time we're conditioned to expect that happiness only exists for children or fools who are out of touch with the real world. Marsha, I wonder if we could explore how it might be possible, even in the most difficult situations, to find happiness. Is it possible, as the subtitle of your book *Living Happily Ever After* implies, to create our own trust, luck and joy? There you seem to be saying, as in your other writings, that maybe the source of our happiness exists at a deeper level, that how we envision our lives may indeed become the world we experience. You suggest that we can create a world where problems become opportunities and all obstacles are merely new challenges to exercise our creative power and bring out our best.

MARSHA: As I wrote *Living Happily Ever After,* I became fascinated with the content of certain fairy tales. I've reviewed some classic tales, given to us before the time of written language—stories from the oral traditions—and I found lessons, passed along from generation to generation, telling us that it is possible to actually have things work out for the good.

MICHAEL: In the book you often referred to the Hansel and Gretel story, in which two young children are sent out into the world on their own, where they confront certain trials and tribulations and eventually come out okay.

MARSHA: Yes. I used Hansel and Gretel as my subtext because it is an archetypical tale. We find similar themes in all cultures, so in that sense it has elements of being mythical, a universally instructive teaching story.

The story describes two young children (as anyone who has read Hansel and Gretel knows) who are thrown out of their home and sent into the world to fend for themselves. They have many adventures as they confront the unknown. Although they face numerous challenges—some of them life-threatening—they overcome them, eventually return home, and live happily ever after.

In a way, the story of Hansel and Gretel is totally contemporary. Here we find a boy and a girl—representing gender differences—from what today we would call a dysfunctional family. Their abuse comes from the hand of their cruel stepmother, and in the end their father reprimands his wife and welcomes his children back into the fold.

The stepmother makes two tries to get rid of the children. The first time, she takes them out into the woods and attempts to lose them. But the children scatter bread crumbs and find their way back by following the trail they've left. The second time out, however, the crumbs are eaten by birds and the children are lost—can't find their way back home.

At this point, lost and alone, the children must face facts and deal with the inevitable—that they are truly abandoned and must utilize their own resources, and each other's help, if they are to survive. This is a lesson for all of us—reminds us of those times when life forces us to bite the bullet and face some task we have been avoiding.

MICHAEL: This is when the children encounter the witch.

MARSHA: Yes, but first they encounter their aloneness and their hunger. What intrigued me most about Hansel and Gretel was the psychological dimension—how the children evolved and ultimately found solutions. Initially, the witch came across as a friend, a good parent figure who gave them all kinds of wonderful goodies to eat and promised them lovely beds and brought them into her perfect, warm little cottage. They were in bliss. And then one thing leads to another and they realize that, here again, their good news turns out to be bad. They soon discover that the old witch is planning to eat them. The old witch represents the demons and trials we all face in our lives, and this suggests that often things are not as they appear.

In confronting this challenge, Hansel and Gretel take turns helping each other out. At different points in the story, each one exhibits strength. And each one exhibits weakness at different points. They have no difficulty expressing themselves, articulating what they feel, and have no trouble asking one another for help. I thought this very touching—the quality of their interdependence, their supportive relationship is a model for us all.

To me, Hansel and Gretel represent the sort of people who manage to live happily ever after. People seem to fall into two distinct groups—the first say they want a certain kind of life. They say they want to be self-actualizing, do work that they love, and so on. But they have a thousand excuses for why they can't. Obstacles for them are not just obstacles but solid walls, preventing them from going on. You know, "The world is against me; I must feed my family, put my kids through college," or "I don't have the right degree," or whatever. Then there's the second group of people, who are wholly different.

The second group celebrates their intrinsic ability to confront the different challenges of life... and most of them are actually doing something they love. Obstacles seem to dissolve before them, not because they are avoiding them or because they are so lucky that they simply don't encounter any problems but because of how they perceive their lives. These are individuals who have developed their innate resources so sufficiently that when a problem arises they see that problem as a teacher, not as a jailer. They don't perceive the problem as yet another sign that the world is against them. These hardy types represent people from all age groups. They are not necessarily affluent but they could be. Money is irrelevant. The thing they all share in common is their celebration of what I call "personal entrepreneurship." Hansel and Gretel are members of this second group, of course; they are personal entrepreneurs.

MICHAEL: You once used the phrase the "creative adaptive response." Is this part of the picture you are describing?

MARSHA: Yes. The creative adaptive response is our ability to look at an obstacle, a difficulty, in an almost objective or humorous way—even when it's something serious like loss, illness, financial problems. It's our capacity to look at our demons and say, I know that I can find the light, a solution, an answer; if I apply myself courageously, with the right focus, with right-mindedness, I'll not only find my solution to this problem but I'll discover a larger truth, a bigger piece of the universe, that can enrich and enlarge me as a human being.

MICHAEL: As I look over the books you have written— starting with *Ordinary People as Monks and Mystics*, then *Do What You Love, The Money Will Follow*, then *Elegant Choices, Healing Choices* and finally *Living Happily Ever After*—I'm wondering how your books reflect your own journey, your own life.

MARSHA: As much as one can ever know one's own motives, I suppose my first three books are a set, a non-fiction trilogy about spiritual emergence. *Ordinary People as Monks and Mystics* has to do with spiritual values, with being born again and encountering the small deaths that occur as we grow toward personhood. Then we begin to appreciate the beauty of existence, even as we see the lies and the seductions that are an unwholesome part of the world. Then *Do What You Love, The Money Will Follow,* my second book, is about healthy vocational patterns. It's for the person who wants to find a livelihood compatible with their values. The third book, *Elegant Choices,* is about conscious choice, for the same self-actualizing person. So the three books together are a whole expression. And in a very real way they describe a personal journey and one that we all face as humans. From the loss of innocence and our discovery of the world into which we've been born, to our choice of a fulfilling livelihood that truly supports us (not just financially but in emotional ways) and finally to our realization that if we are to have the good life we truly want we must learn how to make conscious choices.

In the third book, *Elegant Choices* (as well as in the book I'm currently working on), I attempt to support people who have heard the call to live more consciously but who often feel stuck between the seductions of the world and their desire to be true to themselves. You know, like the career woman who longs to have a family but also feels very nurtured by her career and can't see how she is going to have both. Or the man who paints beautiful canvases in his spare time and works in an office in the city during the week.

There are so many points throughout our lives where we're free to choose to express the very best in ourselves—embrace our virtues through our actions and our will—or choose against our virtue, oppose the best in ourselves. And that is currently what interests me a great deal in my life...

how I might recognize and make those virtuous choices when the opportunities arise. To be able to do so seems the essence of living happily ever after. Perhaps the good life is simply a matter of learning to make these virtuous kinds of choices.

MICHAEL: Isn't the idea of living happily ever after a bit Pollyanna-ish?

MARSHA: Yes, the phrase is Pollyanna-ish. I am trying to get us to take a closer look at the phrase, to see that we adults have a kind of cynicism about that idea because perhaps we've been disappointed, or were not correctly taught what the phrase actually means. Living happily ever after does not mean you're going to be problem-free for the rest of your life. Rather, living happily ever after means that we are "resource-full," "solution-full," not friction-less. Our inner resources let us perceive problems either as great impediments—as restrictions that are going to shape our lives regardless of our wishes—or as opportunities for self-mastery, illumination, God-consciousness.

I propose that if we want to live happily ever after we have to look at problems in a new way. We have to "re-parent" ourselves and change the mentality that says we can't live the life we want. We must unlearn certain erroneous lessons, habits, even belief systems that we learned in childhood.

There are so many adults who are bitter. Life hasn't turned out as they'd hoped it would. In writing *Living Happily Ever After*, I tried to bring readers with me by using the story of Hansel and Gretel as a kind of metaphor to illustrate how we misinterpret the phrase "happily ever after." I thought if I could put that phrase in a different context, people might realize that we really can live happily ever after. We do have this gift of life! And we can celebrate our lives from this day forward.

MICHAEL: Marsha, I bet if we went out on the street and asked ten different people to define happiness we'd get ten different answers. And this suggests that happiness is in the eye of the beholder, that we each define it for ourselves. Some might say that happiness is having a new car. Some might say it is living in a fine house. Others might say it is the freedom to travel, to see and experience far away places, and so on.

MARSHA: When we are happy we have an indwelling bubbling-up of life which is joy. And this joy exists despite external conditions. I know, for example, that it is possible to experience a great loss, a crisis, maybe even be suffering a life-threatening illness, yet still have a grateful heart—a joy in being alive. That's a happy person. Happiness is an end product of right living. Now how do we find language to express that? Happiness is not something you can buy like a new car. Rather it is something that we possess within ourselves. This is the ultimate happiness, a fulfillment, a quality of deep gratefulness, for want of other words, an ecstatic joyousness.

MICHAEL: We can contrast this with many of the social values we are taught, that happiness has something to do with material goods and externals.

MARSHA: In the earlier stages of our development, most of us did equate happiness with getting our first car, our first girlfriend or boyfriend, our new dress, new suit or whatever. But later on, as we have grown and have gained some wisdom, most people have begun to realize that happiness isn't going to emerge from material things but from something deeper, richer and more enduring. If you asked people on the street as you suggest, almost everybody would agree that this is true. So maybe happiness is, after all, something more than in the eye of the beholder; perhaps we should say it is in the heart of the beholder.

MICHAEL: I am reminded here of a phrase you used in one of your books. You said, "Don't dream it, be it."

MARSHA: I remember hearing that for the first time when I was a teenager, and it was such an exciting thought to me, that instead of just dreaming about things I could be them. And I've been working that out, in one way or another, ever since. The more I look at it, think about it, and read and reflect about it, the more I see the truth in it. Our dreams are only the beginning.

MICHAEL: What about people who say, "Oh, yeah, I can dream but it's impossible to do it. I couldn't possibly leave my job," or "I've got a family to raise," or "it's fine for people who don't have responsibilities..."

MARSHA: We all do this to some extent. That is the reason we need to talk about skills—to learn how to liberate ourselves so we don't feel similarly trapped. You know, Michael, as I look around at the United States, I see people who are convinced that they are trapped and that's a great pity. It's not necessary to be stuck. But it does take some doing—that is, a certain kind of courage and skill—to get out of our traps.

MICHAEL: But isn't there another part of the picture to look at? It's hard to deny that many people have lost their jobs because of automation and now we've moved into the information age, moving further and further away from industrial working conditions. What about this? There are certainly many people who don't have any work, who are trapped in the way that the job or profession they've been trained for all their lives simply doesn't exist any more.

MARSHA: Yes, but as I have said, we can create our work. You and I have essentially created our work. And I know young people who have created theirs. They started little businesses for themselves. I also have testimonies of hundreds of people who have been in just the situation you described, automated out of their jobs or whatever. And there's no denying that workers are losing jobs in this country. An industry like steel or computers goes bankrupt or some company is bought out or a person gets ill and can no longer do the kind of work they have always done. And yet, many of them re-tool—re-train themselves. However, to do this they must be willing to move forward.

I write about two attitudes: entrenchment and non-entrenchment. These terms come out of the work of Profes-sor Robert Sternberg at Yale, who has researched learning and creative, problem-solving abilities. Sternberg describes the non-entrenched mind as one that "floats" above problems, that has a certain objective detachment and is thus able to see solutions. These are the sorts of people who go on to create jobs and new lives for themselves. They take action and they do live happily ever after. By contrast, someone with an entrenched mind sees only the problem. You know, "I work on an assembly line and that is all I do. If the assembly line goes away for one reason or another, I am doomed. There is nowhere for me to go." And this is what we must change, move from entrenched thinking to non-entrenched thinking.

MICHAEL: So, in many ways, you are suggesting that living happily ever after requires a certain level of creativity, that we aren't just robots who are programmed in one way, for a particular job or way of life, but that we can develop the ability, the skills, to literally create the worlds we want or the reality that is going to work well for us at any given time. In regard to this, you once said something I thought was very interesting, that optimism is essential to the creative process. Perhaps we could discuss this?

MARSHA: Oh, definitely. You know, in his book *Optimism*, Lionel Tiger writes that he doesn't know what drives ballet dancers to practice day after day until their limbs are numb from pain; but it certainly isn't pessimism. I guess I take that exact stance and say, I don't know what drives any of us to go forward, toward a greater or more fulfilling experience of life, or to reflect what is more fundamentally good or virtuous or brave—but it certainly is not pessimism.

It's important that we not consider optimism or pessimism simplistically—these are not just black and white attitudes. This isn't simply thinking that things are either going to work out or they're not going to work out. There are many colors and shades of optimism and pessimism. The big question is: Are you optimistic enough to live—to put one foot in front of the other? Willingness to be engaged with our lives, that's the key. Are you willing to sit and do your meditation? Are you willing to move out—inch out—into robust work? Are you willing to consider that other job or that better life? And so, it all begins with our willingness.

MICHAEL: I just had the realization that nature herself is optimistic, that perhaps it is a force in us that we all have because we are part of nature. I have an image in my mind of an old highway, one that has been abandoned and is no longer in use because a new one has been built to replace it. Then, on the old highway, a few years later, you suddenly discover flowers are pushing up between the cracks. It seems like proof of nature's eternal optimism.

MARSHA: Yes, that's such a lovely analogy. Let me make an additional point—that the opposite of optimism is depression, not pessimism...

MICHAEL: That reminds me of something the Dalai Lama said. He said that pessimism makes human beings depressed and no human being wants to be depressed. Better to be optimistic.

MARSHA: It's so simple! And you know we make a big fuss about all of this. We write books about optimism and joy and living happily ever after. But really, if you look at a child twirling around, you see that he or she is just becoming dizzy with joy. That's as far as we need to look for what happiness is. It's our ecstatic gratefulness at being alive. It's not that complicated. We ourselves complicate matters by our intellectualizing—we tell ourselves this or that is wrong, or this or that must happen, or "I must have this or that before I can be happy." That's nonsense. It's just mind-chatter. Happiness is, as someone said, just a breath away.

MICHAEL: What do you think is the role of traditional religion in teaching us about happiness? It seems to me that in most religions there is a great deal of emphasis on not being able to achieve happiness in this lifetime.

MARSHA: I would agree that much contemporary religion, particularly as taught by lesser teachers, communicates misery—the sense that we're ill-deserving of happiness. If you look at the great spiritual teachers, they say something totally different. I was recently reading Meister Eckhart's work and then afterwards I went to the shelf and picked up a book of Martin Buber's. As I read Buber's work, I thought for a moment that I was reading Meister Eckhart. They both spoke of the same ecstatic sense of unity consciousness that is, to them, a universal aspect of spiritual enlightenment. When you examine their remarks closely, you see very little difference between one great theologian and another. They are all lovers; they are all singing the praises of their God, Whoever their God is.

MICHAEL: So you really have to go beyond the normal trappings of the religious institution to find the underlying spiritual meanings and this link between spiritual ecstasy and happiness.

MARSHA: Yes. One reason I emphasize autonomy and independent thinking is that we must abandon institutional thought and find our own path. To avoid being crushed by traditional constructs—institutionalized teaching pervades life in school, religion, sociology, politics, whatever—we have to become independent thinkers, able to separate what we're being asked to think from the truth of our own direct experience. One helpful set of traits to develop is what psychiatrist Robert Linder, in his book *Prescription for Rebellion*, calls "positive rebellion." Positive rebels don't resist or fight outside forces, persons or institutions. They don't say, "I must prove that person or that institution wrong before I can have what I want." Rather, they clearly sense what they need and they move toward it, seeing obstacles as challenges—not as limitations to their lives.

I'm reminded of a woman who told me that she feels she has autonomy and high self-esteem now because when she was a child being abused by her parents and her grandparents, she made a firm decision not to respect anybody who did not respect her. And because she made that conscious decision—which for a small child shows tremendous autonomy—she grew up to be a strong, capable, healthy human being.

Once, while I was a guest on a radio talk show, a man called in to say how—when he was ten or so—he made a promise never to lie to himself. He said that he has lied to others, but never to himself. Today, as an adult, he feels pretty good about himself. It's this intention or conscious decision that we will not be taken in or crushed by authority—be it parent, teacher, employer, government, religion or other external forces—that makes us "positive rebels."

MICHAEL: You have said in your books that high self-esteem is an indication, or maybe a prerequisite, for growth towards autonomy and toward the making of the positive rebel. You also speak of the inter-relatedness of self-esteem, expanding one's resourcefulness, and autonomy...

MARSHA: Yes. And these qualities all mesh together like gears. If we feel positively toward ourselves, we can be pretty sure that we'll grow toward resourcefulness. Our resourcefulness—the use of our inner resources, our ability to respond positively in the present—is a key for building personal autonomy.

MICHAEL: Are you suggesting that everybody should just do their own thing, like we used to say in the 60s? Wouldn't that be a kind of anarchy?

MARSHA: Well I don't have a sense that if healthfully autonomous people did their own thing it would be anarchy. I believe that the interests of the greater good are generally recognized and served by wholesome self-interest, which is a key aspect of the healthfully autonomous person. There is, I know, a widespread fear that when individuals find themselves this might somehow be catastrophic for the community. However, the fact is that the opposite is true: that there is nothing worse for the community than a human being who is imploded, constricted and turned against himself. This is the antisocial person, the violent person, the abuser. Abraham Maslow said: "Let us recognize every person who is kind, helpful, decent, psychologically democratic, affectionate and warm as a psychotherapeutic force (for good) even though a small one." In other words, the expression of these higher values in one single individual is healing for the whole community. This idea is important—that as we become more whole we become forces for the greater good. It's in everyone's best interest to develop along these lines and to support that progression in others.

MICHAEL: To use an everyday metaphor, then, it would be like when you get up on the wrong side of the bed and you take that out into the world. In effect, everybody you meet along the way is going to be affected by your condition. Whereas, if the opposite is true, if you go into the world with joy and happiness and optimism, that also affects the people you meet.

MARSHA: Yes. And you know, many successful people I have met over the years seem to radiate, as if they have an inner sun… and it's their love, their warmth, their positivity that everyone around them experiences and warms up to. They can't enter a room without improving it. No wonder they're so successful! We need them.

You know, if you talk to artists about these topics, and you discuss how they work, you'll find that spirituality is *the artist* very much a part of their creative process. And by spiritual- ity I mean the higher values we've been discussing here today and the whole thrust of living happily ever after. Often I'll be talking to an artist or a poet who is not necessarily reli- gious, but who speaks of celebrating life and honoring what's real. To me, this seems enormously spiritual. I find that these same life-enhancing values become alive in their work. They understand that sacred aspect of their work immediately. It's a beautiful thing.

As we turn the corner into the new millennium we're going to see a great mutual support between the arts, the sci- ences and community leadership. If we look at some of the more progressive ways of teaching people with, say, learning disabilities, we already find theater is used, music is used, art is used in drawing out people's best. And art is one of the most effective therapies to help people cope with loss after war or trauma. This is not to say that verbal, cognitive psy- chology is not useful. It is just to say that we need a rich mix to help people help themselves.

MICHAEL: Joseph Campbell spoke of following your bliss and that when we do this we are forced to look inward, to deal with the dark side of ourselves. And it seems to me we are also forced to confront the dark side of the world around us. So doing what you love, following your bliss, isn't all love and light. It's not Pollyanna-ish, airy-fairy living. It has a lot to do with integrity and honesty and authenticity, as you've said.

MARSHA: I agree. Joseph Campbell and many others who speak convincingly of the creative process necessarily show by their lives that they are living authentically. They are honest with themselves about their own experience. If a life is authentic in this way, we'll see texture, shadings, shadows along with the light. And if we observe deeper, we see that it's just magical thinking to believe that we're going to decide to do something and then, the next day, it's going to be done. The point is that we have to learn something in our process of achievement, to grow in the process, to dig a little deeper into ourselves, to bring out something of ourselves that's richer. Well how do we do that? We don't do it by lying in bed all day or by avoiding everything that's unpleasant in ourselves or the world. I mean, even Jesus struggled at times— convincing people, being threatened. That's not to say we make the struggle a way of life, a religion, but that effort is part of our human experience. Life's not always easy. There may be many sacrifices. And somehow, that is also the fun of it!

MICHAEL: And there aren't any guarantees.

MARSHA: Exactly. The only people with guarantees are six feet under. This guarantee is that their material body will stay there unless we dig it up—at least until it decomposes.

MICHAEL: I wonder, doesn't all this looking for guarantees, this questioning the validity of following your vision, your bliss, this seeking security instead... all of this involves the thinking mind, the intellect. And that is what often inhibits us from taking the risk, making the jump, living out there with nothing to hold onto. On several occasions, you have used the term "beyond thinking." How do we do that? How do we get beyond thinking? What exactly is it?

MARSHA: The Zen Buddhists would call this "big mind, open mind." It's a space where the logical mind cannot go. From this place many insights and answers come, answers we don't expect, revelatory answers. And they help us in our most desperate times. This is the mind we need and want. Yet, many scientific thinkers caution us away from the big mind, the open mind. They sound like foghorns warning us out of the deep water where there are no guarantees, into the harbors where there, presumably, is safety and security. The too-linear thinkers are always ready to give us a million reasons why they are right, and it's hard to argue with them, since they so strongly believe they're right.

One thing I've learned is that you can't convince other people that anything of much value can come from this place of consciousness, of no guarantees, or what Alan Watts called walking on the edge. It's difficult to talk about this wisdom of insecurity. It is a vulnerable, transparent place, there's no denying that.

If a person is resistant to this notion, don't waste your time trying to sell them on the idea. But for those who can listen, who are willing to take the risk, who do question and possibly act—people who are willing to put one foot in front of the other and get started on life's true path—these are the people I will talk to and support. One of the best arguments in favor of the wisdom of insecurity is to look at peak experiences, examine times when we feel most vital, most alive. This generally is not when everything is all buttoned down and tidy and secure. This is moksha-liberation; a free-fall into grace.

MICHAEL: I would agree that a lot of the most alive periods I've had in my life have been times that involved some danger.

MARSHA: Yes, I remember something you described a long time ago. You were on a trip and you heard the cry of a peregrine falcon and you heard a wildness to it. And you resonated with its cry. I empathized with you because, as you know, I live in the forest and have been listening to the sounds of the birds for years. My point is not that we are completely wild but that there is a place in us that is free, untamed—and from that untamed place we find such luxuriant possibilities. When everything is all buckled down, you know, when we're not taking life-enhancing risks, and when we are putting too much effort into searching for guarantees, it's almost as if we imprison that wild part of ourselves.

This imprisonment makes us ill. It destroys us when we are unable to acknowledge and express this untamed part of ourselves. Recently I read that about ninety percent of the dolphins in captivity have ulcers. And I cannot help but think that when we are captured, trapped in jobs we don't like, our wildness is suppressed, and we get ulcers, or some other disease, just like dolphins. Children ought to be taught how to avoid being imprisoned. They ought to be taught how to make choices that will bring joy, that let them keep that wild part of the self alive.

Father William McNamara writes about that fiery inner core that can consume us until we're fully alive. This is what I'm talking about—our wild, surprising inner life.

I've also noticed that people who think for themselves, who live their truth with their actions as well as their words—can experience a tension between themselves and most other people. Our surprises frighten others. It unnerves people to see another person free. We must ask ourselves why.

MICHAEL: Well, I think it has a lot to do with sharing an accepted reality. If you don't share the accepted reality you threaten those who cling to that reality for their security.

MARSHA: Yes, and that threat may come from not fully believing that we can live happily ever after—and that it is through our own actions that we do this. To do this we must have a completely regenerated heart, mind and spirit. We must transform our view of life. This is called metanoia. I find many indications throughout our culture, throughout

Hope

our world, that suggest that the whole world is in the process of a transfiguring metanoia—the realization that we really can live wholesomely is spreading.

MICHAEL: You mean that we are entertaining a sort of universal optimism about ourselves?

MARSHA: That's right. I mean there is a collective insight about all this, of living happily ever after—that as each of us changes, passes through our own metanoia we are, in effect, altering those around us. We are serving each other and in doing so, we contribute to this planetary metanoia—a collective aliveness that is slowly spreading throughout the world.

Biographical Notes on Marsha Sinetar

Marsha Sinetar, Ph.D., one of the foremost exponents of the practical value of self-actualization, is an author, educator and corporate psychologist with an extensive background in both education and management. In her private practice, Sinetar specializes in organizational psychology and corporate "change management." She has written numerous articles in the areas of management and leadership psychology. Her books include:

Ordinary People as Monks and Mystics (Paulist Press, 1986)

Do What You Love, The Money Will Follow (Dell, 1989)

Elegant Choices, Healing Choices (Paulist Press, 1988)

A Person Is Many Wonderful, Strange Things (Paulist Press, 1990)

Self-Esteem Is Just an Idea We Have About Ourselves (Paulist Press, 1990)

Living Happily Ever After (Dell, 1990)

Developing a 21st-Century Mind (Villard, 1991)

A Way Without Words (Paulist Press, 1992)

Reel Power: Spiritual Growth Through Film (Triumph Books, 1993)

If you are interested in receiving information on upcoming seminars, or Marsha's latest newsletter, please send a business-sized SASE to:

Marsha Sinetar

Post Office Box 1

Stewarts Point, CA 95480

Biographical Notes on Michael Toms

Michael Toms is recognized as one of the leading spokespersons of "new paradigm" thinking. His perspective has been influenced greatly by his work with the late Joseph Campbell and Buckminster Fuller. He is perhaps best known as the host and executive producer of the widely acclaimed and award-winning "New Dimensions" national public radio interview series. He is Chairman Emeritus of the California Institute of Integral Studies, and currently serves as Senior Acquisitions Editor with HarperCollins San Francisco. His previous books include the bestselling *An Open Life: Joseph Campbell in Conversation with Michael Toms* and *At the Leading Edge: New Visions of Science, Spirituality and Society.*

About New Dimensions

Inspired by the need for an overview of the dramatic cultural shifts and changing human values occurring on a planetary scale, New Dimensions Foundation was conceived and founded in March 1973, as a public, nonprofit educational organization. Shortly thereafter, New Dimensions Radio began producing programming for broadcast in Northern California. Since then, more than 4,000 broadcast hours of programming intended to empower and enlighten have been produced. In 1980, "New Dimensions" went national via satellite as a weekly one-hour, in-depth interview series. More than 300 stations have aired the series since its inception, and "New Dimensions" has reached literally millions of listeners with its upbeat, practical, and provocative views of life and the human spirit.

Widely acclaimed as a unique and professional production, New Dimensions Radio programming has featured hundreds of leading thinkers, creative artists, scientists and cultural and social innovators of our time in far-ranging dialogues covering the major issues of this era. The interviews from which this book was compiled are representative. As interviewer and host, Michael Toms brings a broad background of knowledge and expertise to the "New Dimensions" microphone. His sensitive and engaging interviewing style as well as his own intellect and breadth of interest have been acclaimed by listeners and guests alike.

New Dimensions Radio provides a new model for exploring ideas in a spirit of open dialogue. Programs are produced to include the listener as an active participant as well as respecting the listener's intelligence and capacity for thoughtful choice. The programs are alive with dynamic spontaneity. "New Dimensions" programming celebrates life and the human spirit, while challenging the mind to open to fresh possibilities. We invite your participation with us in the ultimate human adventure—the quest for wisdom and the inexpressible.

For a free *New Dimensions Journal*, including a list of radio stations currently broadcasting the "New Dimensions" radio series, or an audio tape catalog, please write New Dimensions Radio, Dept. SB, P.O. Box 410510, San Francisco, CA 94141-0510; or you may telephone (415) 563-8899.

New Dimensions Tapes with Marsha Sinetar

Daily Life as Spiritual Exercise with Marsha Sinetar.
This is an inspiring and relevant dialogue about being true to one's deepest motivation. Choosing a lifestyle which blends inner truth with daily life is possible, according to Sinetar, who has interviewed many everyday people living unconventional, simple, yet rich and satisfying lives. She emphasizes the importance of solitude, silence and self-awareness for following the spiritual path.
Tape #2007 1 hr. $9.95
Members' price: $8.46

Right Living and Making Money Too! with Marsha Sinetar. Living your dream and following your heart are possible for anyone willing to engage life with passion, according to Sinetar, an organizational psychologist who has studied many people who have become successful doing what they love. Self-esteem, overcoming resistance, accepting and forgiving oneself, taking risks and more are addressed in this visionary yet practical view of merging life and work. The mainstream definition of success undergoes a considerable metamorphosis in this dialogue.
Tape #2041 1 hr. $9.95
Members' price: $8.46

Whole Living: Creative Choices with Marsha Sinetar.
Making life-supporting choices through paying attention to the results in one's life lies at the core of this dialogue with psychologist Sinetar, who gently reminds us to honor our own capacity for knowing. Emphasizing the positive and stressing the importance of accepting what life brings, she reveals a myriad of ways to choose to live in fullness and with joy. For anyone seeking to choose wisely and improve the quality of life, there is much offered here.
Tape #2134 1 hr. $9.95
Members' price: $8.46

Don't Worry/Be Happy with Marsha Sinetar. Using the Hansel and Gretel myth as a metaphor for life, psychologist and writer Sinetar speaks to those who are attempting to live their deepest calling in the midst of a seductive world. Happiness begins on the inside and does not depend on externals or material things, according to her. She emphasizes the power of a positive view without being Pollyanna-ish, and stresses how optimism is essential for the creative process to unfold.
Tape #2199 1 hr. $9.95
Members' price: $8.46

You are a vital part of the work we do!

Please become a member of "Friends of New Dimensions."

We encourage you to become a member of "Friends of New Dimensions" and help bring life-enhancing topics and ideas to the airwaves regularly. As an active member at the individual level or higher, you will receive:

- *New Dimensions* newsletter/journal, a quarterly publication containing feature articles and interviews spotlighting some of the same people and ideas you hear on our radio program, up-to-date program listings for the entire country, descriptions of new tapes, music and book reviews, and items of special interest to New Dimensions listeners.

- A 15% discount on all purchases made through New Dimensions.

Your membership contribution makes it possible to bring life-enhancing topics and ideas to the airwaves regularly, so please join at the level most consistent with your life- or work-style.

Use the order form on the following page. ⇨

New Dimensions Order Form

(U.P.S. cannot deliver to P.O. box)   Date _____

Name _____

Address _____

City _____ State _____ Zip _____

Phone _____

Please send a catalog to my friend:

Name _____

Add/City/St/Zip _____

Tape #	Qty.	Title	Amount
2007		Daily Life as Spiritual Exercise with Marsha Sinetar	
2041		Right Living and Making Money Too! w/Marsha Sinetar	
2134		Whole Living: Creative Choices with Marsha Sinetar	
2199		Don't Worry/Be Happy with Marsha Sinetar	
	1	Tape Catalog	FREE

Check type of payment:
☐ Check or money order ☐ Visa ☐ MC
(payable in U.S. funds)

_____

Acct. #

_____

Exp. Date

Subtotal	
Sales Calif. res. 7.25% Tax BART counties 7.75%	
Shipping & Handling	
Membership	
Total	

Signature—required for all credit card purchases

☐ **YES!** I want to support the radio work
and become a member of "Friends of
New Dimensions." I understand this enti-
tles me to a 15% discount on all purchases from New Dimensions.

☐ Individual $35 (S721)   ☐ Radio Council: $250 (SP 72)
☐ Family: $45 (S721)   ☐ Satellite Sponsor: $500 (SP59)
☐ Sustaining: $50 (SP94)   ☐ Benefactor: $1000 (SP95)
☐ Radio Underwriter: $100 (S726)

Send order to:
New Dimensions Tapes
P.O. Box 410510
San Francisco, CA 94141-0510
Or order by telephone:
(415) 563-8899
with VISA or MasterCard
ANY TIME, DAY OR NIGHT

SHIPPING & HANDLING

If subtotal falls between	add:	
	U.S. & Canada	Foreign
0-$15.99	$2	$6
$16-$30.99	$4	$8
$31-$50.99	$5	$10
$51-$70.99	$6	$12
$71-$100	$7	$18
over $100	$8	$25

All domestic orders are shipped 1st Class mail or UPS.
All orders going outside the U.S. are shipped air.
FOREIGN ORDERS: Please send an international
bank money order payable in U.S. funds, drawn
through a U.S. bank.

OUR GAURANTEE: All New Dimensions tapes
are unconditionally guaranteed. If for any reason
you are dissatisfied, you may return the tape(s)
within 30 days of purchase for a full refund or
exchange.

Allow one to three weeks for delivery.

Upcoming Books in the New Dimensions Series

Fritjof Capra in Conversation with Michael Toms

edited by Hal Zina Bennett
In this book, Fritjof Capra takes us with him on his remarkable personal journey into the nether realms of quantum physics, where the traditional worlds of science and spirit twist and merge to the point where the distinctions become blurred. As he relates his wisdom-packed interactions with some of the leading contemporary thinkers and visionaries, from Gregory Bateson to Krishnamurti, we discover with him new ways of thinking and being.

$8.95

$8.95

Lynn Andrews in Conversation with Michael Toms

edited by Hal Zina Bennett
Shamaness Lynn Andrews takes us into the wilderness of self to plumb the depths of our heart so that our being can soar. Her vision quest journey has taken her from the wilds of Manitoba to the jungles of Yucatan and the Aboriginal outback of Australia, as she attempts to bridge the gulf between the primal mind and contemporary life. In this book, she challenges us to see the infinite range of possibilities that lies beyond our ordinary limits—personal and planetary.

Patricia Sun in Conversation with Michael Toms

edited by Hal Zina Bennett
Patricia Sun is an extraordinary teacher, human energizer and natural healer. In this book she shows how to become more aware of your intuition, and so become more trusting of the Self. With gentle directness, she encourages us to live with spontaneity, continually receptive to the creative force within us. As our words and feelings become aligned with the source of great wisdom within, we assist in the birth of a new world of harmony, cooperation and love.

$8.95

Other Books from Aslan Publishing

✶ Gentle Roads to Survival

by Andre Auw, Ph.D.

This is one of those rare, life-changing books that touches the reader deeply. Drawing from his forty years of counseling as a priest and a psychotherapist, Auw points out the characteristics that distinguish people who are "born survivors" from those who give up, and teaches us how to learn these vital skills. Using case histories, and simple, colorful language, Auw gently guides us past our limitations to the place of safety and courage within.

$10.95

The Heart of the Healer

edited by Dawson Church and Dr. Alan Sherr

Bernie Siegel, Larry Dossey, Norman Cousins and sixteen other healing professionals here intimately describe their vision of the healing process and the innermost workings of the true healer. An inspiring and definitive review of the emerging holistic paradigm in healing.

$14.95

✶ Intuition Workout

by Nancy Rosanoff

This is a new and revised edition of the classic text on intuition. Lively and extremely practical, it is a training manual for developing your intuition into a reliable tool that can be called upon at any time—in crisis situations, for everyday problems, and in tricky business, financial, and romantic situations. The author has been taking the mystery out of intuition in her trainings for executives, housewives, artists and others for over ten years.

$10.95

Live Your Passion

by Lynne Garnett, Ph.D.

Live Your Passion is a job and career book for the next phase of the economy. It is focused not on "getting a job" or "climbing the corporate ladder," but doing what you most love as a career path. Practical and down-to-earth, this outstanding book contains dozens of worksheets, exercises and visualizations that allow you to find your deepest purposes—and then actualize them in work.

$10.95

Other Books from Aslan Publishing

Living At the Heart of Creation

by Michael Exeter

Author Michael Exeter is one of the most important voices today for the emerging field of eco-spirituality. *Living At the Heart of Creation* pierces beyond the superficial fixes to the most pressing problems of our day. Blending profound spirituality with wide ecological knowledge, it offers remarkable insights into such challenging areas as the environmental crisis, business, relationships, and personal well-being, inspiring us to live at the heart of creation.

$9.95

Magnificent Addiction

by Philip R. Kavanaugh, M.D.

Kavanaugh's revolutionary work is decisively changing the way we see addictions and emotional disorders. Our unhealthy addictions aren't bad, he says—and it's a waste of time and effort to get wrapped up in getting rid of them, as he demonstrates in his own wrenching personal story. We simply need to upgrade our addictions to ones that serve us better, like addiction to wholeness, life, spontaneity, divinity.

$12.95

Personal Power Cards

by Barbara Gress

An amazing tool for retraining the negative emotions that sabotage most attempts at recovery and personal growth, *Personal Power Cards* work scientifically through colors, shapes and words to re-program the brain for maximum emotional health. Called "One of the most useful recovery tools I have seen" by *New Age Retailer,* these are a simple, incredibly quick and effective technology for building a powerful sense of self-worth in a wide variety of life areas.

$18.95

When You See a Sacred Cow... Milk It for All It's Worth!

by Swami Beyondananda

The "Yogi from Muskogee" is at it again. In this delightful, off-the-wall little book, Swami Beyondananda holds forth on the ozone layer, Porky Pig, Safe Sects, and the theology of Chocolate. Read a few lines and you'll quickly realize that nothing's safe from his pointblank scrutiny.

$9.95

Aslan Publishing Order Form

(Please print legibly)   Date _____

Name _____

Address _____

City _____ State_____ Zip _____

Phone _____

Please send a catalog to my friend:

Name _____

Address _____

City _____ State_____ Zip _____

Item	Qty.	Price	Amount
Fritjof Capra in Conversation with Michael Toms		$8.95	
Lynn Andrews in Conversation with Michael Toms		$8.95	
Patricia Sun in Conversation with Michael Toms		$8.95	
Gentle Roads to Survival		$10.95	
The Heart of the Healer		$14.95	
Intuition Workout		$10.95	
Live Your Passion		$10.95	
Living At the Heart of Creation		$9.95	
Magnificent Addiction		$12.95	
Personal Power Cards		$18.95	
When You See a Sacred Cow, Milk It...		$9.95	

Add for shipping:
Book Rate: $2.50 for first item, $1.00 for ea. add. item.
First Class/UPS: $4.00 for first item, $1.50 ea. add. item.
Canada/Mexico: One-and-a-half times shipping rates.
Overseas: Double shipping rates.

Subtotal	
Calif. res. add 7.25% Tax	
Shipping	
Grand Total	

Check type of payment:

☐ Check or money order enclosed
☐ Visa   ☐ MasterCard

Acct. # _____

Exp. Date _____

Signature _____

Send order to:
**Aslan Publishing
PO Box 108
Lower Lake, CA 95457**
or call to order:
(800) 275-2606

NDMS

Aslan Publishing Order Form

(Please print legibly)   Date _____

Name _____

Address _____

City _____ State_____ Zip _____

Phone _____

Please send a catalog to my friend:

Name _____

Address _____

City _____ State_____ Zip _____

Item	Qty.	Price	Amount
Fritjof Capra in Conversation with Michael Toms		$8.95	
Lynn Andrews in Conversation with Michael Toms		$8.95	
Patricia Sun in Conversation with Michael Toms		$8.95	
Gentle Roads to Survival		$10.95	
The Heart of the Healer		$14.95	
Intuition Workout		$10.95	
Live Your Passion		$10.95	
Living At the Heart of Creation		$9.95	
Magnificent Addiction		$12.95	
Personal Power Cards		$18.95	
When You See a Sacred Cow, Milk It...		$9.95	

	Amount
Subtotal	
Calif. res. add 7.25% Tax	
Shipping	
Grand Total	

Add for shipping:
Book Rate: $2.50 for first item, $1.00 for ea. add. item.
First Class/UPS: $4.00 for first item, $1.50 ea. add. item.
Canada/Mexico: One-and-a-half times shipping rates.
Overseas: Double shipping rates.

Check type of payment:

☐ Check or money order enclosed

☐ Visa   ☐ MasterCard

Acct. # _____

Exp. Date _____

Signature _____

Send order to:
Aslan Publishing
PO Box 108
Lower Lake, CA 95457
or call to order:
(800) 275-2606

NDMS